SEWING VINTAGE
STYLE

SEWING VINTAGE
STYLE

MARY JO HINEY

Sterling Publishing Co., Inc. New York
A Sterling/Chapelle Book

CHAPELLE, LTD.

Owner: Jo Packham

Editor: Karmen Quinney

Staff: Areta Bingham, Kass Burchett, Ray Cornia,
Marilyn Goff, Karla Haberstich, Holly Hollingsworth,
Susan Jorgensen, Emily Kirk, Barbara Milburn,
Cindy Stoeckl, Kim Taylor, Sara Toliver,
Desirée Wybrow

Historical Text: Caroll Shreeve

Photo Stylist: Jill Dahlberg

Photography: Kevin Dilley for Hazen Photography

Library of Congress Cataloging-in-Publication Data

Hiney, Mary Jo.
    Sewing vintage style / Mary Jo Hiney.
        p. cm.
    "A Sterling/Chapelle book."
    Includes index.
    ISBN 0-8069-2697-X
        1. Fancy work. 2. Decoration and ornament. 3. Vintage clothing.
        4. Household linens.
    I. Title.
    TT751 .H57 2002
    746--dc21   2002030399

10 9 8 7 6 5 4 3 2 1

A Sterling/Chapelle Book

Published by Sterling Publishing Co., Inc.
387 Park Avenue South, New York, NY 10016
© 2003 by Mary Jo Hiney
Distributed in Canada by Sterling Publishing
% Canadian Manda Group, One Atlantic Avenue, Suite 105
Toronto, Ontario, Canada M6K 3E7
Distributed in Great Britain by Chrysalis Books
64 Brewery Road, London N7 9NT, England
Distributed in Australia by Capricorn Link (Australia) Pty. Ltd.
P.O. Box 704, Windsor, NSW 2756, Australia
Printed in China
All Rights Reserved

Sterling ISBN 0-8069-2697-X

Due to the limited amount of space available, we must print our patterns at a reduced size in order to give our patrons the maximum number of patterns possible in our publications. We believe the quality and quantity of our patterns will compensate for any inconvenience this may cause.

If you have any questions or comments, please contact:

Chapelle, Ltd., Inc.
    P.O. Box 9252
    Ogden, UT 84409
    Phone: (801) 621-2777
    FAX: (801) 621-2788
    e-mail: chapelle@chapelleltd.com
    web site: www.chapelleltd.com

INTRODUCTION

*W*e are learning to simplify our lives and reward ourselves with comfort and style on any budget. The most adventurous of style trends is exemplified by the creative recycling and transformation of vintage objects into tasteful treasures we can enjoy today.

The marriage of the practical with the beautiful is apparent in the handcrafts of those who labored for hours with needle and thread, embellishing linen, silk, velvet, satin, everyday cotton, and muslin. The legacy they left us in vintage clothing and household items is—in most cases—imperfect or in shreds.

Precious fragments of the past offer exquisite lace, frayed petticoats, ribbon roses, and crochet-edged table and bed linens. Transform them, as Mary Jo Hiney explains, into home and wearable "art," perhaps by copying old patterns. Share her passion for the well-loved and the dilapidated-but-beautiful details in classic handcrafts refashioned into stylish echoes of their once-grand elegance.

Contents

VINTAGE SEWING
-8-

VINTAGE QUILTING
-44-

VINTAGE NEEDLEWORK
-68-

STITCHES
-118-

TRANSFERRING
-124-

ACKNOWLEDGMENTS
-126-

METRIC CONVERSION CHARTS
-127-

INDEX
-128-

Vintage Sewing

grew. Tatted, knitted, or crocheted lace insertions, or fine drawn work were added vertically, horizontally, or diagonally. They followed a row of tucks in perfect parallel. Dart tucks formed little bias triangles to radiate a flair effect from a starched collar, a lacy sleeve, or to give extra fullness at yoke or waist.

From early times, hand-sewn clothing items were fashioned for beauty and usefulness. Stitches were counted by threads often on "pulled thread" rows for uniform perfection. Ladies' dresses were elegant with pleats, ruffles, tucks, and folds sewn into the material that varied from no wider than a needle to a width of more than 2". Tucks were not just for beauty but for strength and, when it came to the length of a sleeve, skirt, or shirt, they could be "let out" as children

Sewing Tool Keeper

In days gone by, fine sewing tools were precious commodities. Their availability might mean not only modest expense, but catalog orders transported by ship or train over long distances, waited for in terms of weeks or even months. Keeping needles and pins sharp and sewing tools in good order was part of the admired-seamstress role aspired to by wise homemakers. Many needlework tools became treasured heirlooms for daughters' dowries.

Instructions

1. For tool-keeper front, cut 11" square from olive green linen. For tool-keeper back, use pillowcase, including decorative edge. Cut 11" x 12" piece from linen for back.

2. Cut two 3" squares, two 3⅛" x 6½" pieces, one 2¾" x 6¼" piece, and one 2½" x 3" piece from embroidery scraps, utilizing finished or decorative edges. *Note: If you have a finished edge to work with, you will not need the ½" seam allowance for a side or a bottom; you will not need the 1" pocket-facing allowance for tops.*

Continued on page 12.

Materials

Grosgrain ribbon: *½"-wide, vintage chartreuse (1 yd) for tool-keeper tie*

Linen: *44"-wide, lt. olive green (⅓ yd) for tool-keeper front*

Matching threads

Vintage embroidered scraps: *assorted (6) for pockets*

Vintage pillowcase with decorative edge: *white ivory, 11" x 12" for tool-keeper back*

Tools

Fabric scissors

Iron with steam/ironing board

Point turner

Sewing machine

Straight pins

Continued from page 10.

3. To make pocket facing, turn top edge of pocket under ¼" and machine-stitch close to edge along fold from wrong side.

4. Fold and pin facing to right side of pocket ¾" from stitched edge. Stitch ends with a ½" seam allowance. Clip bulk from corner and trim seam to ¼". Edge-press seam open.

5. Turn facing right side out and using point turner, push out corners. Press unfinished edges under ½", keeping bottom corners square. *Note: If an edge already has a decorative finish, it is not necessary to press under these edges.*

6. Position pockets on tool-keeper front as shown in Diagram A at right. Stitch each pocket along side and bottom edges. Press well.

7. For decorative top flap, use a 3" x 11" embroidered scrap. Following Step 3, make a pocket facing on flap. Pin and stitch top edge of flap over three top pockets.

8. Fold ribbon length in half and pin to center-left edge of tool keeper.

9. Pin wrong side of back to right side of front, positioning decorative finished edge of back with bottom edge of front. Stitch sides and top edge, taking a ½" seam allowance. Clip bulk from corners and trim seam to ¼". Edge-press seam open. Turn right side out. Press and edge-stitch all edges. *Note: If a raw corner from back piece shows on the front side along bottom edge, tuck in raw edge before edge-stitching.*

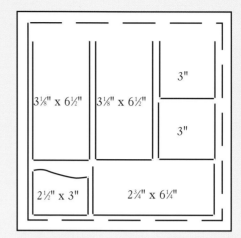

Diagram A

VINTAGE SEWING HUTCH

BABY SHOE PINCUSHION

elebrate a child's birth or first birthday with a commemorative pincushion that harkens back to the 17th century. No couple did without one or many as gifts for their newborn in the days of symbolic gift giving. Pins were precious commodities and decorative heads on pins made them even more valuable in a tuffet designed for a loved one.

MATERIALS

Button: *1", mother-of-pearl*

Clear glass hearts with embedded wire hangers: *⅜"-wide (9)*

Crescent board: *2" x 8"*

Embroidery floss: *gold metallic*

Lace trim: *½"-wide (½ yd)*

Linen or muslin scrap: *white*

Old leather baby shoe

Papier-mâché or chipwood round box: *1½" dia. Note: Make certain box fits into shoe.*

Polyester stuffing

Silk brocade ribbons: *1"-wide, off-white (⅝ yd); 1½"-wide, ecru (7")*

Thread: *white*

Vintage lace: *2" squares (2)*

Vintage pearl clasp

TOOLS

Craft scissors

Fabric scissors

Hand-sewing needle

Industrial-strength glue

Tacky glue or hot-glue gun/glue sticks

VINTAGE PINCUSHION

INSTRUCTIONS

1. Stuff toe of shoe with stuffing to give shape. Cover box bottom and side with white fabric. Using industrial-strength glue, glue box bottom and sides to inside of shoe back and sides. Box lid will not be used.

2. Thread 1"-wide ribbon through lace-up eyelets. Wrap ribbon around shoe, then tie ends into a bow to one side. Trim ends.

3. Using two strands of gold floss, stitch glass hearts to 1"-wide ribbon through imbedded hangers, spacing hearts about ¾" apart.

4. Cut four 1¼" circles from crescent board. Glue circles together, forming inner lid. *Note: Make certain circle fits inside box. Trim if necessary.* Cut 4" circle from white fabric. Gather-stitch around outer edge of circle. Place inner lid onto center of fabric circle, then pull stitches as tightly as possible so that fabric cups around inner lid. Secure stitches. Trim excess fabric if necessary.

5. For pincushion lid, cut 1⅝" circle from crescent board. Fold 1½"-wide ribbon in half, right sides together, aligning short ends. Taking ¼" seam allowance, sew across ends, forming a circle. Finger-press seam open. Turn right side out.

6. Using tacky glue or hot glue, glue one selvage edge onto outer edges of lid, easing ribbon to fit as necessary. When glued in place, the piece will resemble a fabric "cup" with a crescent-board bottom.

7. Gather-stitch around top selvage edge of fabric cup. Do not cut thread. Stuff cup firmly with stuffing, then pull stitches as tightly as possible to close opening. Secure stitches.

8. Using tacky glue or hot glue, glue edge of lace trim around outer edges of lid on wrong side of lid.

9. Glue top of inner lid to bottom of lid, forming pincushion. Glue lace squares to bottom of pincushion.

10. Using industrial-strength glue, glue mother-of-pearl button to bottom of pincushion. Glue pearl clasp to center top of pincushion.

VINTAGE PINCUSHIONS

Pincushions have graced virtually every sewing table. In the 17th century, decorative handmade pincushions, also known as pin keepers, pin poppets, and tuffets, were used to express messages of love and personal significance. Stuffed with granular or fibrous components such as paper, bran, sawdust, emery powder, unraveled knitting or crochet, and woolen fibers, pincushions let us peek into a bygone era. The tinkling bell at the door of the couturier's shop announced the arrival and departure of daily patrons. Fine gentlemen and fashionable ladies examined the latest styles in the converted tea parlor where textiles, scented of distant lands, sat stacked from rug to rafters. Between these fabricated cliffs, the sheerest laces spilled to the floor, mixing with rattan baskets, treasured notions, trinkets, and threads.

Observing all—amid dress forms, hat boxes, tapes, and scissors—a quiescent pincushion reposed on the mantle. Close at hand, the fat tuffet of velvet poised in a silver dish guarded a myriad of sharp, shiny pins and needles.

VINTAGE TUFFETS

*S*hop around at vintage or used clothing stores for an old, sheer blouse that has some type of pleated fabric application. The fabric can be sheer tricot or organza chiffon. A slip with a double flounce will work terrifically for a long rectangular pillow. Pillow size will be determined by the size of the blouse or slip, so be flexible with size and be ready to make the pillow in a size that is not standard.

MATERIALS

Corner of a vintage handkerchief

Pillow form: *10"–14"*

Print fabric: *muted (¼–½ yd)*

Satin ribbon: *⅝"–1"-wide (1 yd)*

Vintage sheer-fabric blouse or slip, with pleated ruffles or flounce

Vintage or silk rose

TOOLS

Fabric scissors

Iron/ironing board

Sewing machine

Straight pins

Tape measure

INSTRUCTIONS

1. Determine the size of pillow you can make from blouse. Trim blouse pillow front to size (11" square for a 10" pillow; 13" x 15" for a 12" x 14" pillow, etc.). *Note: For long rectangular pillow, cut fabric 9" x 21".*

2. Cut front lining fabric the same size as pillow fabric. Pin front to lining.

3. For pillow backs, cut two pieces of fabric so backs can overlap approximately 1" onto each other. Allow for a hem along one edge. *Note: For a 10" finished pillow, cut back pieces 8" x 11". For a 12" x 14" finished pillow, cut back pieces 10" x 13". For an 8" x 20" finished pillow, cut back pieces 9" x 13".* Along center back edges, press fabric under ½" to wrong side. Press fabric again over on itself ½" to wrong side.

4. Cut length of satin ribbon in half. Pin one end of ribbon to center of inner pressed edge, then machine-stitch hem in place, catching ribbon end at same time. Machine-stitch second hem. Press hemmed edges. Working with second piece, mark center of edge opposite hemmed edge. Pin one end of second piece of ribbon onto mark.

5. Working from fabric's right side, overlap pillow backs so they match up to the size of pillow front. Pin overlaps in place.

6. Overlay pillow front onto pillow back. Pin in place with right sides facing. Stitch around the four edges, taking a ½" seam allowance. Trim bulk from corners and edge-press seams open before turning pillow right side out.

7. Insert pillow form. Use ribbons to close pillow back. If the bow is tied along the top edge of the pillow, the silk flower can be slipped through the ribbon. Otherwise, the flower stems can be hand-stitched to pillow front.

HEIRLOOM-SLIP PILLOW

Enhancing the beauty and comfort of clothing and household items with pleats and ruffles remains nearly as popular as it was in the past.

Pleating by carefully tucking even amounts of fabric at a waistband, for example, and securing it with stitching, means that the additional material below that secured area will be heat-pressed into a crisp pleat, rather than allowing the fullness to fall freely from a gathered band.

Pleating can be a relief embellishment, as in fan-like attachments, to beautify boxes, hats, and so forth.

Ruffles are long, hemmed strips of straight or bias-cut fabric that are added to curtains, skirts, sleeves, collars, by first gathering them for fullness and pinning them in place, then rolling and whip-stitching them on by hand or attaching them by machine.

ORGANZA PINTUCKED PILLOW

An easy way to create the tucked-fabric pieces needed for a pillow or garment is to make tucked "strips" the lengths of the pattern pieces required. Then, lay the patterns on top of the pretucked strips and cut them out, stitching around the edges to hold the tucks in place, before assembling with other pattern pieces to make the garment.

Project Tips:

- When working pintucks and ¼"-deep tucks, begin with a piece of fabric that is larger than needed. After tucks have been stitched, trim fabric down to correct size for pillow.

- Pintucks are more successful and dramatic when worked on a starched or stiffened lightweight fabric, such as organza used for this project.

- Read your sewing machine manual for working with a pintuck foot and ready the machine:

  Insert pintuck foot into machine.

  Swap needle for twin needle.

  Place thread in bobbin.

  Using two spools of thread, thread the two needles.

  Change thread tension as suggested in sewing machine manual.

  Remove needle plate so that gimp thread or kite string can be threaded upward through hole in needle plate.

  Return needle plate to its position. Rest gimp thread or kite string near machine while sewing.

- Pintucks are quite easy to stitch. Practice on a 5" x 9" piece of fabric until you have a comfortable feel for how your machine and fabric will react.

- Practice pintucks:

  Using water-soluble pen, draw a straight line in center of fabric scrap.

  Stitch first tuck directly on marked line, then trim threads.

  Move fabric to the right ⅛" so a pintuck foot groove sits on top of first tuck. Stitch, keeping foot groove on tuck. Trim threads.

Move fabric to the right another ⅛" Set pintuck foot groove on second tuck. Stitch, then trim threads.

Move fabric ⅛" to the left of first tuck and position foot groove so that it sits on top of first tuck. Stitch as before, then trim threads.

Move fabric ⅛" to the left again, position groove, stitch and trim threads. This completes a set of five pintucks. Spray fabric with water to remove pen markings. Crisply press tucks.

After several sets of five tucks have been completed and pressed, you will notice that the fabric shape becomes a little warped. This is why the fabric is worked as a lager piece, so that it can be trimmed perfectly square to the proper size needed.

FRENCH SEAM

1. Stitch seam line, taking a ¼" seam allowance. Trim seam allowance to ⅛".

2. Press seam allowance toward one side. Fold fabric along seam line, right sides together, and press. Pin and stitch, taking ¼" seam allowance.

MATERIALS

Assorted buttons: *⅜"–⅝", mother-of-pearl (5) for center section*

Matching threads

Organza fabric: *44"-wide, off-white (1 yd) for front and back*

Pillow form: *14", or polyester stuffing*

Ribbon: *⅞"-wide, sheer white (1 yd) for back ties*

Toile: *beige print (½ yd) for sheer sections and pillow insert*

TOOLS

Cutting mat

Fabric scissors

Fray preventative

Hand-sewing needle

Iron with steam/ironing board

Point turner

Press cloth

Rotary cutter

Sewing machine/accessories:
  Bobbin thread to match or contrast
  Cord/pintuck foot
  Gimp thread or kite string
  Twin needle: size 2mm/80

Spray bottle/water

Straight pins

Tape measure

Transparent ruler with gridlines

Water-soluble pen

INSTRUCTIONS

Note: The patterns for the Organza Pillow are simple rectangles. It is not necessary to photocopy these patterns. Rather, use the measurements given to cut and mark fabric.

1. Cut pillow fabric.

a. For ¼" tuck (referred to as Section A), cut organza 9" x 25"; for pintuck (referred to as Section B), cut organza 9" x 19"; for center front (referred to as Section C), cut organza 4" x 15"; for back (referred to as Section D), cut two 9" x 15" pieces from organza. The back section is also part of pillow front side edges.

2. Make ¼" tucks on Section A fabric.

a. Using water-soluble pen, center and mark fold lines onto fabric as shown in Diagram A on page 22.

b. Fold fabric on first fold line and press. Stitch ¼" from fold to make first tuck.

Note: Your sewing machine foot may be sized to stitch a perfect ¼" seam. If not, determine where ¼" is from the needle position and make a mark. Align fold with ¼" mark. An alternative is to change the needle position or change to a foot that makes a perfect ¼" seam.

c. Fold fabric on second fold line, press, then stitch ¼" from fold. Continue to fold, press, and stitch tucks in this manner.

d. Spray fabric with water to remove pen markings. Crisply press left folds toward left and right folds toward right.

e. Using cutting mat, rotary cutter, and ruler, trim tucked piece so that it measures 6" x 15", with tucks centered on 15" length. Set piece aside.

3. Make pintucks on Section B fabric.

a. Using water-soluble pen, center and mark pintuck lines onto fabric as shown in Diagram B below.

b. Beginning with center line, make five pintucks: one on mark, two to the right of mark, and two to the left of mark.

c. Beginning with right line, make five pintucks: one on mark and four to the right of mark.

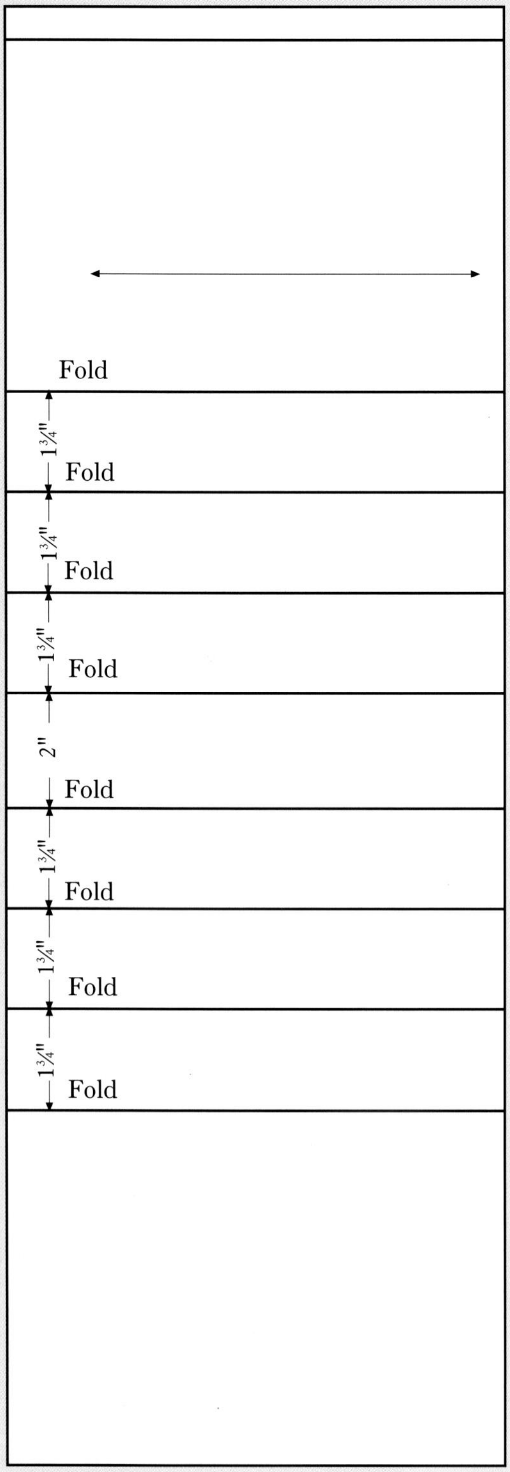

Fold

1¾" Fold

1¾" Fold

1¾" Fold

2" Fold

1¾" Fold

1¾" Fold

1¾" Fold

Diagram A—¼" Tuck Section

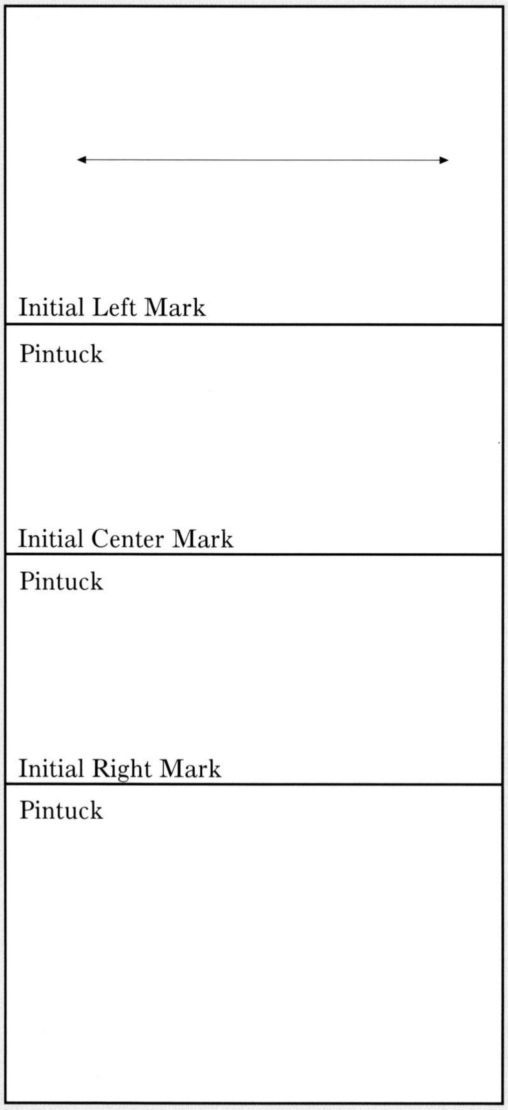

Initial Left Mark

Pintuck

Initial Center Mark

Pintuck

Initial Right Mark

Pintuck

Diagram B—Pintuck Section

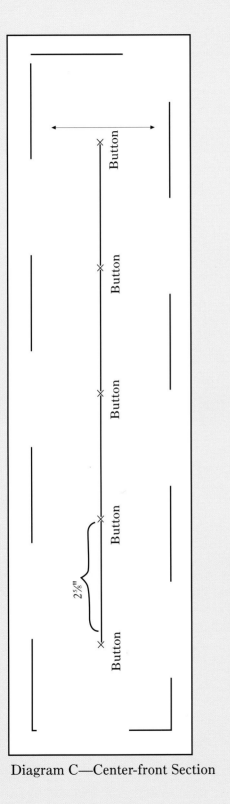

Diagram C—Center-front Section

NARROW HEM

1. Fold raw edge of fabric over ¼" to wrong side. Fold over again and stitch along inside edge of fold, forming a ¼"-wide hem, then press.

d. Beginning with left line, make five pintucks: one on mark and four to the left of mark.

e. Spray fabric with water to remove pen markings. Crisply press tucks.

f. Using cutting mat, rotary cutter, and ruler, trim pintucked piece so that it measures 6" x 15", with tucks centered on 15" length.

4. Assemble pillow cover.

Note: The pillow is assembled with French seams as explained on page 20. The French seams create an elegant finish for the sheer fabric.

a. With wrong sides facing, stitch long edge of Section A to long edge of Section C with a French seam. Press finished seam toward Section C.

b. With wrong sides facing, stitch remaining long edge of Section C to long edge of Section B in same manner. Press finished seam toward Section C. Mark Section C for button placement 2⅝" as shown in Diagram C at left. Stitch buttons in place.

Continued on page 24.

Continued from page 23.

c. Mark two pillow Section Ds for ribbon placement as shown in Diagram D at right. Pin ribbons in place on marks, with one cut ribbon edge even with fabric edge. Finish edge with a ¼" narrow hem as explained on page 23, stitching the ribbon in while hemming.

d. Working with unfinished long edge of one Section D, stitch front to back with a French seam as explained on page 20. Repeat with remaining back. Press finished seams toward the back.

e. Fold pillow in half, wrong sides facing, so that backs meet. Stitch with a French seam. Press finished seam toward back.

f. For pillow insert, cut two 14" squares from contrasting fabric. Taper squares inward ½" at each corner. *Note: This eliminates misshapen pillow corners.*

g. Stitch pillow around sides, taking a ½" seam allowance and leaving 7" opening along one edge.

h. Clip bulk from corners. Edge-press seams. At opening, fold over each edge at ½" seam line and press as though opening had been stitched.

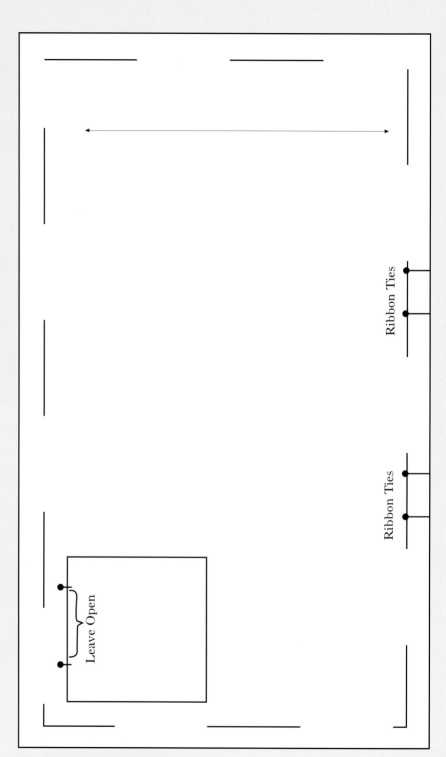

Diagram D—Back Section, cut 2

i. Turn pillow right side out. Using point turner, push out corners. Slip pillow form into fabric through opening. Machine-stitch the opening closed close to edges. *Note: An alternative is to hand-stuff the pillow insert with stuffing.*

j. Slip pillow insert into pillow. Using ribbon, tie backs together. Use fray preventative on ribbon ends.

ANTIQUE PINTUCKED DRESS

Lovely handmade garments, from baby clothes to wedding dresses, were pintucked by seamstresses with an eye for detail. Even young men's dress shirts received such treatment. That pintuck tradition spanned the decades between Victorian times and the 1940s. As in the dress pictured at right, creating a harmonious design by repeating groups of pintucks with spaces between the groups and different numbers of pintucks within each group brought hemline interest high up into each garment. When combined with a lace hem and a smocked bodice, as in this dress, the effect is a memorable heirloom well worth preserving.

DUTCH LAUNDRY SACK

Gone are the days when boys and girls carried sacks to primary school for their art supplies or gym clothes. But here to stay are the practical opportunities for using charming handmade sacks at school, at home, and for traveling. Laundry bags for collecting soiled clothing and transporting it to where it will be washed are not likely to go out of style soon. Designing with Dutch appliqués or other theme icons makes personalizing sacks fun.

MATERIALS

Cord: ¼"-wide, ecru (2¼ yds)

Cotton fabrics: *dk. red print (½ yd) for lining; wide-striped (½ yd)*

Cotton quilting fabrics: *checkered green; solid green; muslin; solid red (¼ yd each)*

Embroidery flosses: *black; golden brown; green brown; red*

Matching threads

Snaps: ⁵⁄₁₆" *(2)*

Vintage dresser scarf with filet-crocheted trim edges: *18" x 50"*

TOOLS

Fabric scissors

Iron/ironing board

Permanent-ink gel pen: *blue*

Sewing machine

Straight pins

Tape measure

Tracing paper

INSTRUCTIONS

1. Cut two 5½" x 11½" pieces from muslin.

2. Cut 3" x 4" piece from solid red fabric. Refer to Transferring on page 124. Using gel pen and Bodice II Transfer Pattern and Stitch Guide on page 28, transfer neckline, sleeve line, and midriff line onto solid red fabric. Using iron, heat-set ink.

3. Refer to Stitches on pages 118–123. Using Outline Stitch, embroider line with two strands of green floss. Using tiny Straight Stitches, fill in bodice space with one strand of green floss.

4. Cut 3" x 4" piece from solid green fabric. Using gel pen and Bodice I Transfer Pattern and Stitch Guide on page 28, transfer sleeve line, then embroider sleeve line with two strands of red floss. Embroider straight lines for buttons.

5. Position bodice piece on muslin. Baste-stitch in place ⅜" inward from design line. Trim excess fabric ¼" beyond design line. Turn edges of bodice fabric under ¼" for a 1" space and invisibly stitch in place with matching thread. Continue to appliqué bodice to muslin in this manner, clipping curves and trimming excess fabric as needed. Appliqué green shirt and red hat in the same manner.

6. Using gel pen and Dutch Girl and Boy Transfer Patterns and Stitch Guide below, transfer pattern onto muslin as shown in Placement Diagram. Using Outline Stitch, embroider dutch girl's and boy's hands, hats, faces, hair, eyes, and eyebrows with one strand of floss. Using Straight Stitch, embroider eyelashes, noses, and mouths with one strand of floss.

7. Cut two 1" x 15" bias strips from checkered green fabric. Seam together and press in half, aligning raw edges. Beginning and ending at bodice bottom edge, stitch bias to appliquéd muslin, taking ¼" seam allowance, pleating bias once at corners to enable bias to turn the corner. Press seam toward bias.

8. Working with second piece of muslin, turn edges under ¼" to wrong side. Place against bias-edged muslin, wrong sides together. Pin in place. Machine-stitch close to bias seam, catching all layers.

9. Stitch one snap side to bottom edge of bodice/shirt.

10. Using Pant Transfer Pattern and Stitch Guide on page 29, transfer and cut out one pant from solid red fabric and one

Placement Diagram

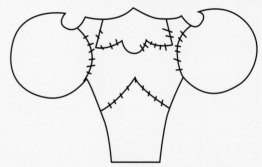

Arm Transfer Patterns

Bodice I Transfer Pattern and
Stitch Guide

Hat Transfer Pattern

Bodice II Transfer Pattern and Stitch
Guide

Dutch Girl and Boy Transfer Patterns and Stitch Guide

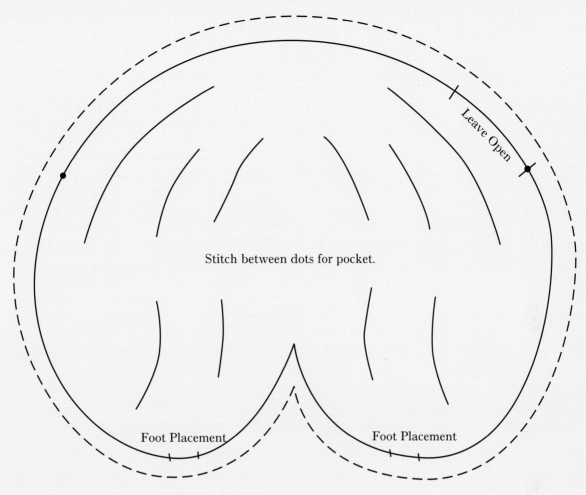

Stitch between dots for pocket.

Foot Placement   Foot Placement

Leave Open

Pant Transfer Pattern and Stitch Guide

pant from muslin. Using Skirt Transfer Pattern and Stitch Guide on page 30, cut out one skirt each from checkered green fabric and muslin. Using Apron Transfer Pattern and Stitch Guide on page 30, transfer and cut out apron from muslin. Using Outline Stitch, embroider apron pockets and hem trim with one strand of floss. Appliqué apron to skirt front. Using Outline Stitch, embroider pant lines.

11. Using gel pen and Foot Transfer Pattern at right, transfer four feet onto double-layered fabric. Using a 1.5-sized stitch, stitch around feet on traced lines. Do not stitch across ankle. Trim seam allowance to ⅛". Clip curves. Turn feet

right side out and press. Position ankle edge of feet on pants and skirt. Pin in place.

Foot Transfer Pattern

12. With right sides facing, stitch muslin to pants, taking ¼" seam allowance and leaving an opening along the side. Repeat with skirt fabrics. Clip seam at curves and inner angles. Clip bulk from corners. Turn right side out through opening. Press. Stitch opposite side of snap to wrong side of pants/skirt at waist.

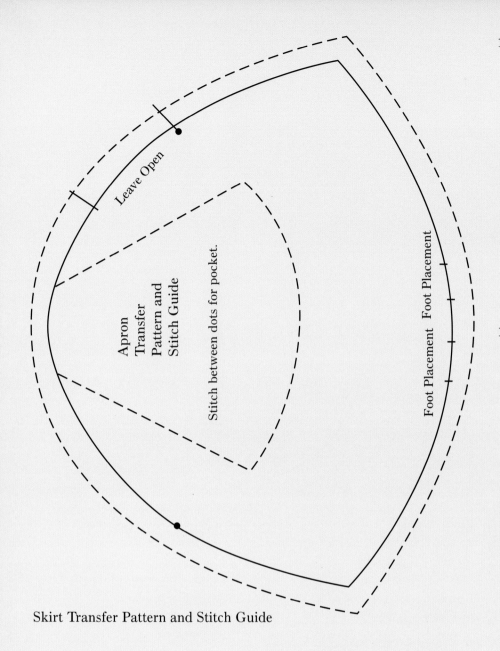

Leave Open

Apron Transfer Pattern and Stitch Guide

Stitch between dots for pocket.

Foot Placement   Foot Placement

Skirt Transfer Pattern and Stitch Guide

15. Stitch bias-edged appliqué piece to large pocket front, placing top edge 2" down from finished top edge of pocket. Machine-stitch sides and bottom edge in place, forming upper pocket. Snap pants and skirt onto shirt bodice. Stitch pants and skirt to large pocket front with matching threads, beginning at dots indicated on pattern, forming smaller pockets.

16. Fold dresser scarf in half, aligning shorter ends, to find the center. Stitch larger pocket to one half of the dresser scarf, aligning raw edge of pocket with center mark, placing raw edge ½" upward from center. Stitch raw edge. Press smaller pocket onto center mark, taking ½" seam allowance with smaller pocket raw edge. Press smaller pocket upward. Make ½"-deep pleat at bottom sides of smaller pocket and pin in place. Stitch smaller pocket sides to the dresser scarf half, over larger pocket.

17. Press ends of dresser scarf over 1" to right side. Stitch 1" from the folded edge, forming casing for cord. Fold dresser scarf in half and stitch the sides together. Insert cord into casing openings from left and right sides.

13. Cut 13½" x 18" piece each from dk. red print and wide-striped fabrics for large pocket. Cut 8" x 13½" piece each from print and striped fabrics for small pocket. Cut 13½" x 18" piece from dk. red print fabric for large pocket lining. Cut 8" x 13½" piece from dk. red print fabric for small pocket lining.

14. Place larger pieces together with right sides facing. Stitch sides and one shorter edge (top of pocket), taking ½" seam allowance. Clip bulk from corners and turn right side out. Press. Repeat with smaller pieces.

EMBROIDERED SUNDRESS

*E*mbroidery of children's clothing, using outline stitches, French knots, and stem and satin stitches, can be beautiful, even when worked in only one color of thread in a simple design. Elaborate lacy edges tend not to ravel out after repeated laundering and years of frequent use.

MATERIALS

Checkered fabric: *lt. green (⅓ yd)*

Cotton sheeting fabric: *white (1 yd)*

Crochet thread: *size 20 or 30, blue*

Embroidery flosses: *aqua; lavender; lt. orchid variegated; white; pale yellow; yellow variegated*

Matching threads

Round vintage tablecloth: *40" dia.*

Vintage crocheted trim: *4" x 12"*

Voile: *off-white (⅓ yd)*

TOOLS

Copy machine

Fabric scissors

Iron/ironing board

Pencil

Purchased toddler's dress pattern

Sewing machine

Steel crochet hook: *size 8*

Tracing paper

1. For bodice front, cut 10" x 14" piece from lt. green checkered and voile fabrics. Place voile over checkered fabric and baste-stitch layers together.

2. Refer to Transferring on page 124. Using pencil and Smiles Transfer Pattern on opposite page, transfer pattern onto center of fabric. Refer to Stitches on pages 118–123. Using Coral Stitch, work lettering with three strands of aqua embroidery floss. *Note: An alternative would be to use vintage embroidered pieces to make the dress.*

3. Cut skirt from embroidered fabric (vintage tablecloth). Stitch scrap pieces of embroidered edges to surround embroidered word. Cut bodice front from surrounded embroidered word. Assemble dress, following pattern instructions, inserting the vintage crocheted trim between the bodice and skirt fronts.

4. Following pattern's instructions, lightly transfer dress pattern onto front of cotton sheeting.

5. Enlarge Floral Transfer Pattern 200% on opposite page. Using pencil, transfer pattern onto dress front and back, going from edge to edge. Draw a scalloped shape along hem edge.

6. Work design onto cotton sheeting fabric. Using Satin Stitch, stitch bow with three strands of white floss. Using Stem Stitch, embroider stems. Using Lazy Daisy Stitch, embroider leaves with three strands of pale yellow floss. Using French Knot Stitch,

embroider flower circles with knots placed closely together with six strands of floss. Press embroidery from wrong side.

7. Using crochet picots, finish scalloped edge of fabric with the blue crochet thread.

Floral Transfer Pattern

Smiles

Smiles Transfer Pattern

CHILD'S NAPKIN APRON

Crocheted edges on embroidered items were practical as well as embellishing features of handwork in the past. Contrasting colors for the edging was considered fashionable and extra "fancy" in its day. A rolled hem, made perfectly even by pulling a thread first, could be pierced with a fine crochet hook at regular intervals of a designated number of threads, and then a combination of picot and scallop stitches would be worked for an edge.

MATERIALS

Embroidery floss

Linen napkin with contrasting crocheted edging

Vintage dish towels, tea towels, or napkins *(2)*

TOOLS

Copy machine

Embroidery needle: *size 3*

Fabric scissors

Pencil

Purchased child's apron pattern

Tape measure

Tracing paper

INSTRUCTIONS

Note: If you have been unable to find a linen napkin with contrasting crocheted edges, alternatives would be to crochet the edges or stitch a narrow crocheted trim to the edges of a linen napkin.

1. Refer to Transferring on page 124. Using pencil and Floral Transfer Pattern below, transfer onto on one corner of linen napkin.

Floral Transfer Pattern

2. Refer to Stitches on pages 118–123. Using Buttonhole Stitch, embroider flowers with two strands of embroidery floss. Using French Knot Stitch, embroider flower centers. Using Stem Stitch, embroider stems. Using Lazy Daisy Stitch, embroider leaves. Using Outline Stitch, embroider lettering. Using appropriate stitch, decorate lettering with flowers and leaves.

3. Refer to purchased pattern. Cut skirt for apron from one towel or napkin. From second towel or napkin, cut waist ties, waistband, bib, and neck ties.

4. Position two corners of linen napkin on bib front. Stitch in place.

5. Assemble apron, following pattern instructions.

TODDLER'S SMOCK

ewing children's clothing is one of the true delights of parenthood. Embellishing each garment with personal loving touches in classic needlework techniques is even more rewarding. Toddlers enjoy pretty things to wear. Adding fancy embroidery, ribbons, pin-tucks, buttons, and beads to their special-occasion and everyday playclothes makes dressing up extra fun for children. Smocks are so cool and comfortable for toddler girls during the summer months that they will beg for several versions and ask to wear them often.

MATERIALS

Buttons: *1", pink (2)*

Cutwork embroidery floss

Embroidered handkerchief for pocket

Matching threads

Patchwork scrap: *5" x 12" (optional)*

Tatted-edged fabric: *4" x 40", or edge from a vintage pillowcase*

Toweling fabric: *18" x 28", or vintage towel, pillowcase with cutwork edges or embroidery, or patchwork scrap*

TOOLS

Copy machine

Fabric scissors

Hand-sewing needle

Pencil

Purchased toddler's smock pattern

Sewing machine

Tracing paper

INSTRUCTIONS

1. Cut smock from worked toweling fabric. Create patchwork or use a scrap of patchwork for bodice front.

2. Hand-stitch corner of embroidered handkerchief to the skirt for pocket.

3. Assemble smock, following pattern directions. Embellish an edge of fabric with tatting or use edge from vintage pillowcase and stitch along skirt bottom edge.

4. Make buttonholes in shoulder straps. Hand-stitch buttons on bodice as indicated on pattern.

5. Enlarge Toddler's Smock Transfer Pattern below 200%. Refer to Transferring on page 124. Using pencil, transfer pattern onto toweling fabric. *Note: Dashes denote the design to be repeated.*

6. Refer to Stitches on pages 118–123. Using Buttonhole Stitch, work edge of the toweling fabric, the three-leaf clovers, and the circles with cutwork embroidery floss. Work entire design along one 18" edge of toweling fabric. Work scallop-edged design along opposite edge of toweling fabric.

Toddler's Smock Transfer Pattern

FANCY FELT PINCUSHIONS

ool fleece will "felt" naturally. The fiber known also as "staple" is constructed by a series of overlapping scales which have a serrated edge. There is a natural elasticity or "creep" to the fiber, caused by the protein keratin. Man-made felt requires the action of four elements: heat, moisture, friction, and pressure. Felt is the oldest form of controlled fabric made by man and predates Christianity. The oldest and finest felt remains that have been found date from around 700 BC. Siberian people made their tents from felt, as well as their clothes and decorations for animals, including saddles. Even ancient armor was made from layers of thick felt and leather, dense enough to resist fire and arrowheads. Felt tents are snow and rain resistant. Felt can also be made from beaver or rabbit fur.

MATERIALS

Cardboard

Polyester filling

Stranded embroidery flosses: *rayon, assorted shades (5)*

Wool-blend felts: *assorted shades (7–10)*

TOOLS

Chenille embroidery needle: *size 18–20*

Electric clothes dryer

Fabric scissors

Pencil

Sewing machine

Sink

Straight pins

Tape measure

Tracing paper

Opposite side of Purse Pincushion

b. Overlap and offset two petals. Refer to Stitches on pages 118–123. Using needle and decorative Straight Stitches, stitch two petals together with three strands of rayon floss. Lightly stuff petal with polyester filling, then gather-stitch ends closed. Repeat with each of eight sets of petals. Do not stuff center petal layer.

c. Join five bottom petals together with doubled thread at gathered edges. Pull thread as tightly as possible and secure thread. Join first petal to last.

d. Roll center petal and secure roll at overlap.

e. Stitch remaining two petals onto top of center of five petals. Stitch rolled petal to center of petals.

f. Offset leaves and using decorative Straight Stitches, stitch together as in Step 1c above for Rose Pincushion.

g. Using two strands of embroidery floss, stitch up through bottom center of rose and to top side of any petal, burying end inside petal. Using Straight Stitch, embroider star. Stitch through petal about ½" and stitch another star. Stitch back through bottom center, then back up to top side of another petal. Continue to stitch stars on each petal.

INSTRUCTIONS

1. Fleece felt.

Note: Before making the rose or felt purse, fleece the felt. The felt must be either a 20% wool–80% rayon blend or a 35% wool–65% rayon blend.

a. Wet felt completely with warm water in a sink or basin. Do not rub or agitate. Wash colors separately, as some may bleed. The felt will shrink.

b. Squeeze by hand to remove as much water as possible. Avoid wringing felt.

c. Place in clothes dryer on regular setting until felt is nearly dry, approximately 35 minutes. Do not overdry.

d. Lay flat to dry completely, smoothing fabric gently by hand.

INSTRUCTIONS FOR ROSE PINCUSHION

1. Make rose from fleeced felts.

a. Refer to Transferring on page 124. Using pencil, trace Pattern A on opposite page onto several shades of fleeced felt. Trace Pattern B on opposite page onto two shades of fleeced felt. Cut out designs.

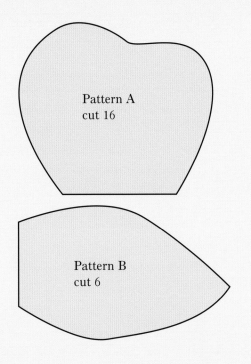

Pattern A
cut 16

Pattern B
cut 6

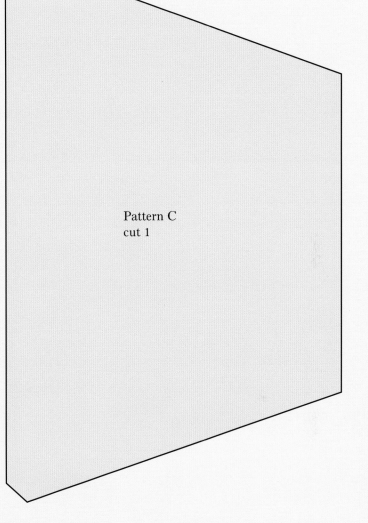

Pattern C
cut 1

INSTRUCTIONS FOR PURSE PINCUSHION

1. Make purse from fleeced felts.

a. Using Patterns C–K on pages 41–43, cut purse pieces from random shades of fleeced felt.

b. For purse front, machine-stitch the left and right Ds together, and stitch the left and right Es together, taking a ¼" seam allowance. Press seams open. Stitch D to E, matching the center front seams and taking a ¼" seam allowance. Press seam open.

c. Center and pin circle H on purse front. Pin moon I over top-left side of circle. Pin flower G and flower center F on top of circle. Using needle and two strands of rayon floss in assorted shades, appliqué moon, circle, flower, and flower center to purse front with decorative Straight Stitches.

d. Pin remaining moon to center of purse back. Pin second flower center to back. Appliqué each to purse back in same manner as Step 1c at left.

e. Stitch J to front, right sides together, matching dots at front bottom edge center and taking a ¼" seam allowance. Stitch side of J to back in same manner.

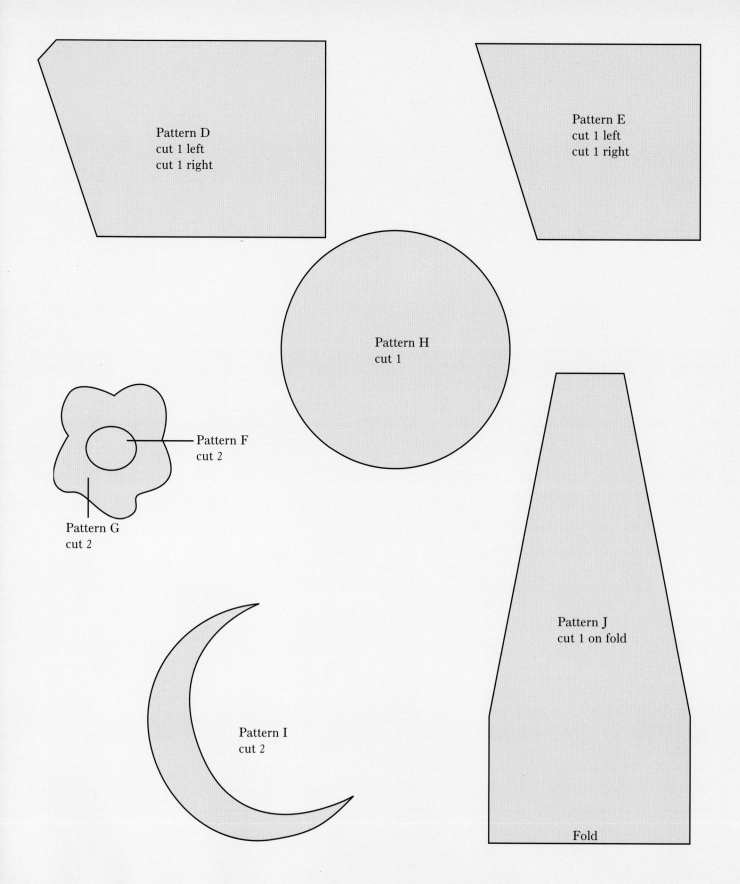

Pattern D
cut 1 left
cut 1 right

Pattern E
cut 1 left
cut 1 right

Pattern H
cut 1

Pattern F
cut 2

Pattern G
cut 2

Pattern J
cut 1 on fold

Fold

Pattern I
cut 2

f. Turn purse right side out. Using decorative Straight Stitches, stitch over front and back seams at sides with three strands of rayon floss.

g. Cut 1" x 5" strip from felt for top band. Using decorative Straight Stitches, hand-stitch top band to purse front with three strands of rayon floss.

h. Cut three pieces of cardboard to fit inside purse bottom. Glue cardboard together. Place inside purse.

i. Firmly stuff purse with polyester filling.

j. Using decorative Straight Stitches, hand-stitch back of top band to purse back with three strands of rayon floss.

k. Fold one handle K in half, matching long edges. Beginning and ending 1" from each end, machine-stitch handle ⅛" from fold. Trim excess fabric from machine-stitched edges. Trim each end into a small circle. Repeat for second handle.

l. Using Crisscross Stitches, appliqué handles to purse front and back at each circle with two strands of rayon floss.

Pattern K
cut 2

You just get some wool fleece off a sheep, spread it out on a sheet, fold the sheet over it, wet it and jump on it. It's what happens to a sweater in the washing machine, but the wool doesn't have to be knitted or woven first.

—Kay Donald,
Creative Feltmaking

Vintage Quilting

There was a time when no hope chest was complete without at least one quilt for every day and, if the young bride-to-be were fortunate, another painstakingly made showpiece quilt that her mother may have helped her piece and finish. The art of quilt making has evolved in purpose from the days of providing necessary warmth in as beautiful a style as possible. Quilts, quilted pillow tops, and even quilted clothing are as intricately designed and stitched, or more so, than the ones our foremothers made. New fabrics, fill fibers, and technology, not to mention revolutionary attitudes about creativity, have launched a flurry of quilt interest.

Many quilters use traditional designs made up of precise squares or triangles; others prefer creating complex appliqués from patterns or their own plans. Selection of fabric colors and patterns is no longer constrained by the scrap box. Quilts have taken on focal-point status in home living areas, rivaling their importance in the past. As bed covers, wall hangings, and pillows, quilts are back—happily here to stay.

Crazy-quilting is an old needle art form that has a new following among quilt lovers. Visual feasts and textural delights are its mainstays. Velvets and silks, denims and twills, satin and toile, you'll find them all combined in shimmering colors and encrusted with every imaginable embellishment. Ribbon roses, buttons and beads, embroidered pansies and intricate cretan stitches enhance a potpourri of shapes, colors, patterns, and textures. Crazy-quilting brings out the adventurous risk taker in a needle artist who may even create wild items with photo-portrait transfers to wear on children's or adults' vests, and tote bags.

CRAZY-QUILT SEWING CASE

*M*ismatched and faded fabrics are the height of fashion when it comes to crazy-quilting and fabric collage. Sometimes the tonal nuances of aging fabrics, threads, and yarns add just the subtlety needed for a special project with a well-loved appearance. Fabric collage and crazy-quilting are extremely popular techniques today for aesthetic as well as political tribute pieces planned for large-scale public display. These two techniques are quite often seen in unique wearing apparel that may be of museum quality.

MATERIALS

Assorted items for crazy-quilted and collaged top

Batting

Brocade trim: *1⅛"-wide (1¼ yd)*

Buttons: *large (2)*

Crazy-quilted or foundation-pieced quilt blocks *(4)*

Crescent board: *30" x 40"*

Cuff from old blouse

Fabric ribbon scraps

Muslin *(½ yd) for foundation*

Old jewelry *(2 pieces)*

Old slip with pleated flounce

Polyester filling

Ribbonwork flowers *(4–6)*

Sequins by the yard *(⅓ yd)*

Sewing machine charm

Silk brocade fabric *(½ yd)*

Small vintage train case or hat box *Note: Ours is 13"-square. Papier-mâché train cases are available, if you can't find an old one.*

Taffeta ribbon: *3"-wide, plaid (1 yd)*

Tapestry fabric *(¼ yd)*

TOOLS

Disposable paint roller: *3"-wide*

Fabric scissors

Industrial-strength glue

Iron/ironing board

Hot-glue gun/glue sticks

Pencil

Sewing machine

Tacky glue

INSTRUCTIONS

1. Trace top and bottom of train case onto crescent board. Cut out and set aside.

2. Cut a fabric strip from tapestry that will wrap around lower side of train case (below zipper if there is one) and 1" onto bottom. Using tacky glue and disposable paint roller, glue tapestry to lower side and bottom of train case.

3. Cut flounce from slip and press under upper trimmed edge so that it has a clean finish. Hot-glue pressed-under edge to lower side of train case, just above tapestry top edge. (Be certain to leave enough clearance for zipper.)

4. Cut a piece from muslin that is 1" larger all around than crescent-board top.

5. Start collage by arranging crazy-quilted squares and fabric scraps on muslin foundation. If there is a leftover piece of flounce from slip, include it. When pleased with arrangement, stitch pieces in place, working with the crazy-quilting technique of flip and stitch.

6. Arrange remaining goodies on fabric piece, then hand-stitch in place. *Note: Some pieces can simply be tied, glued, or pinned in place.*

7. Hot-glue a piece of batting to one side of crescent-board top, then snugly wrap fabric top around crescent board. Trim away fabric bulk from underside. Hot-glue wrong side of top to train case top, working quickly.

8. Using tacky glue and disposable paint roller, glue 1⅛"-wide brocade trim to upper lip of train case, leaving enough clearance for zipper if there is one. *Note: Trim can be applied with fusible webbing.*

9. Cut another piece from tapestry to fit back of train case that will "hinge" top to bottom, allowing an additional ½" on each side and 1" on top and bottom. Press under side edges, then glue pressed-under edges in place. Press under top edge. Trim away some bulk, then glue the pressed-under edge in place.

10. Carefully hot-glue "hinge" to back of train case at upper back side edge, at "hinge" location and along sides. Glue excess fabric to bottom of train case.

11. Check fit of crescent-board bottom against bottom of train case. Trim if necessary. Cut a piece from silk brocade fabric ¾" larger all around than crescent-board bottom. Using tacky glue, glue brocade to crescent board, gluing raw edges to underside. Hot-glue wrong side of crescent-board bottom to bottom of train case, again working very quickly. *Note: If using tacky glue, allow additional time for the glue to dry.*

12. Tuck flounce of slip inside case handle, creating festoon effect.

13. Slip 3"-wide ribbon through old handles and tie ends together.

14. Fork-cut ends.

a. Fold desired ribbon in half lengthwise. See (1) below.

b. Cut end of ribbon diagonally from corner point on selvage edge. See (2) below.

c. Completed fork cut. See (3) below.

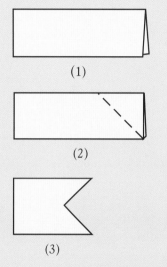

(1)

(2)

(3)

VINTAGE CRAZY-QUILTED FOOTSTOOL

Fiber artists and creative quilters of today combine a variety of fabrics and stitches in fashion accessories. Ordinary as well as metallic yarns and threads, beads, crystals, braids, tassels, and every imaginable trim embellishment are worked into their unique interpretations of the crazy-quilt art.

MATERIALS

Antique trims: *¼"-wide, gold metallic (½ yd); ³⁄₁₆"-wide, gold metallic (2 yds)*

Assorted braid trims: *1½"–2"-wide jacquard (½–¾ yd of 4); scrap (6")*

Assorted specialty beads: *sizes 3mm–5mm*

Beaded flower appliqués *(2)*

Beaded fringe: *¼"-wide, amber (⅓–½ yd)*

Bugle bead: *dk. red*

Fabric for lining *(¼ yd)*

Hex-cut bead: *8/0, celadon green*

Matching threads

Scroll gimp: *¾"-wide for handle (1 yd)*

Seed beads 11/0: *brown; dk. green metallic; olive; matte silver*

Sequined leaf appliqués: *gold (2)*

Vintage lollipop stamens: *dk. brown*

Vintage satin purse: *6" x 9", or smaller*

Wire: *26 gauge*

TOOLS

Beading needle

Hand-sewing needle

Industrial-strength glue

Needle-nosed pliers

Tacky glue

Wire cutters

INSTRUCTIONS

1. Arrange jacquard trims onto purse. When pleased with arrangement, hand-sew onto purse's outer fabric.

2. Accent trimmed edges with metallic trims, beaded fringe, or a line of stitched beads. To stitch beads: Working with doubled thread and beading needle and using the beads in a random fashion, slip needle through back side of braid along selvage at a beginning point. Slide about ½" length of beads onto needle, then slip needle into braid selvage, extending beads flat. Backstitch through several beads, then slide ½" length of beads onto the needle as before until the desired edge has been accented with beads.

3. Hand-stitch vintage stamens to back side of beaded flowers. Using industrial-strength glue, glue beaded leaf and flower appliqués onto purse front.

4. Cut 36" length from wire. Wrap one wire end several times around needle-nosed pliers. Stitch looped wire end to purse at top-left side. Slide an assortment of beads onto wire, working with 4"–5" of wire at a time. Curlicue and loop beaded wire as if doodling, hand-tacking wire to purse at intervals. Wrap remaining wire end several times around needle-nosed pliers, then stitch end to purse front.

5. Hand-stitch ends of the scroll gimp to purse back at frame top for handle.

6. Using tacky glue, glue lining to inside of purse or hand-stitch in place.

Trapunto Boudoir Envelope

The Italian word "trapunto" refers to a version of padded quilting using two layers, but the design is not limited to stuffing between straight lines. For the contemporary fabric artist, a shape stitched with two layers of fabric can be as freeform as desired. Historically, these shapes to be stuffed were often symbols and shapes relating to the Christian church on liturgical vestments for clerics. The higher the office, the more elaborate the design. Embellishing these padded or stuffed forms with fancy stitches, perhaps in metallic threads, then adding beads or sequins and other trims is an art form of its own.

Materials

Cord or string: 1/16"-wide (2 yds)

Flannel: 44"-wide (½ yd)

Lettuce-edged ribbon: 1"-wide (1⅛ yds)

Lightweight fabric, such as organza or voile: 44"-wide (½ yd) for backing

Matching thread

Satin: 44"-wide (1¼ yds)

Vintage silk flowers (2)

Yarn: white

Tools

Copy machine

Fabric scissors

Hand-sewing needle

Iron/ironing board

Pencil

Sewing machine

Straight pins

Tape measure

Tapestry needle

Tracing paper

INSTRUCTIONS

1. Cut two 17" x 12" pieces from satin fabric for front flap and flap lining. Cut two 22" x 16½" pieces from satin fabric for envelope and envelope lining. Cut 1"-wide bias strips from excess satin for a total of 60" in length. The bias strips will be pieced together. Cut one 18" x 13" piece each from backing fabric and flannel. Cut one 22" x 16½" piece from flannel for envelope.

2. Enlarge Trapunto Design 200% on page 54. Refer to Transferring on page 124. Using pencil, lightly transfer design onto right side of satin fabric for front flap.

3. Place backing fabric on work surface, wrong side up. Place satin over backing, right side up. Hand-baste-stitch the layers together.

4. Hand-stitch or machine-stitch design "channels" through layers. Tie thread ends on wrong side of backing.

5. Thread length of yarn into tapestry needle. Insert needle through backing into one end of a channel and carry yarn between satin and backing to the other end. Exit needle at channel end. Trim yarn and tug lightly on channel so yarn ends recede into channel. If it is too difficult to stitch through backing into channel, cut a small slit near ends of a channel in backing. Continue until each channel has been filled with yarn.

6. Place layer of flannel on work surface, right side up. Place trapuntoed fabric over flannel, right side up. Pin layers together.

7. Stitch bias lengths together and press seams open. With bias wrong side up, place narrow cord or string near center

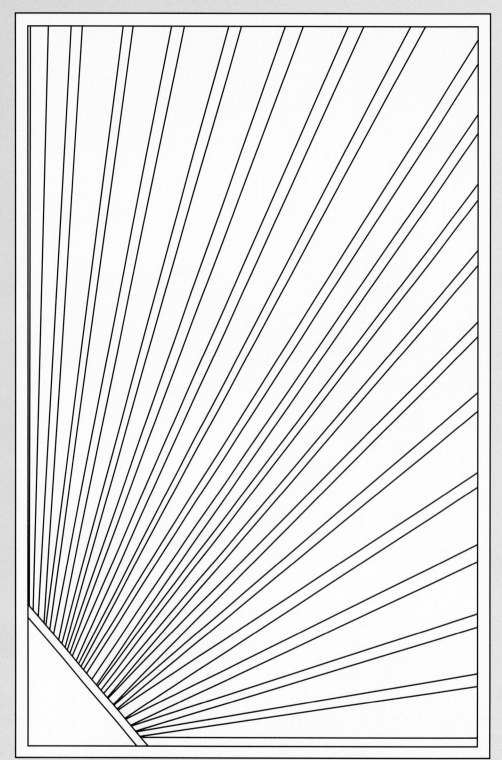

Trapunto Design

of bias. Fold bias over, enclosing cord for piping. With right sides facing, stitch piping to side and front edges of trapunto front, taking a ⅜" seam allowance.

8. Stitch front to front lining along sides and front edges, right sides together, taking a ½" seam allowance. Trim seam allowance to ¼", clip bulk from corners. Edge-press seam allowances, then turn right side out. Press flap flat from lining side.

9. Layer and pin together right side of flannel envelope piece against wrong side of satin envelope piece. Fold layered piece in half, right sides together, aligning 16½" edges. Stitch sides, taking a ¼" seam allowance. Press seam allowance open and turn right side out.

10. Stitch back edge of front flap to back edge of envelope, right sides together. Press seam allowance open.

11. Fold envelope lining in half, right sides together, aligning 16½" edges. Stitch sides, taking a ½" seam allowance, leaving a 4" opening at one side seam. Press seam allowances open and turn right side out.

12. With right sides together, slip lining over envelope/front flap. Have trapunto flap hidden inward. Machine-stitch at top edge with a ½" seam allowance. Trim seam to ¼" and edge-press. Turn envelope right side out through side opening in lining. Press, then machine-stitch top edge of envelope, keeping trapunto flap free. Hand-stitch opening of lining closed.

13. Hand-stitch vintage flowers to top-left edge of flap. Slip books, magazines into envelope. Tie closed with ribbon.

VINTAGE QUILT KITCHEN ITEMS

Salvaging the best portions of a vintage quilt can provide pieces that can be made into coordinated kitchen items such as pot holders, tea cozies, napkins, table runners, toaster covers, coasters, and place mats.

Knitting is not only one of the oldest branches of practical needlework, it has been perfected to the point that inventing new stitches or patterns is nearly impossible. Also called "pins," traditional needles were made of steel, boxwood, or bone. Loops or stitches are usually formed from yarn, using two needles, to produce a whole uncut garment or a knitted piece that can be combined with others. Circular knitting is worked on four or five needles.

Instructions

1. Refer to Transferring on page 124. Using pencil, transfer two of Pattern A onto fuchsia felt and onto mustard felt. Cut two of Pattern A from each color.

2. Cut two ⅝" circles from kelly green felt.

3. Transfer eight of Pattern B onto lt. green felt. Cut eight of Pattern B.

4. Cut four ¼" squares from mustard felt.

5. Transfer four of Pattern C onto dk. red felt. Cut four of Pattern C, four ⅛" x 2" strips, and two ⅛" x 3½" strips from dk. red felt.

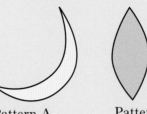

Pattern A   Pattern B

Pattern C

Materials

Embroidery flosses: *black; gold*

Fabric: *17" x 26½" for back of holder*

Felts: *ecru, 14½" x 24"; fuchsia (scrap); green, 8" x 24"; kelly green (scrap); lt. green (scrap); mustard (scrap); dk. red (scrap); tan (scrap)*

Grosgrain ribbon: *½"-wide (1 yd)*

Matching threads

Vintage linen handkerchief

Tools

Embroidery needle: *size 3*

Fabric scissors

Marking pencil: *silver or white*

Scallop-edged scissors: *large*

Sewing machine

Straight pins

Tape measure

Tracing paper

6. Cut two ⅝" circles from tan felt.

7. Working with fabric for back of holder, fold all edges under ¾" to wrong side. Position piece of ecru felt centered on top of back fabric against side with pressed-under edge. Pin in place. Cut piece of ribbon in half and layer two pieces, aligning them at one end. Slip ends in-between felt and back fabric at center of left side. Pin in place. Stitch felt to back fabric as close to edges of felt as possible.

8. Position one corner of handkerchief diagonally centered over ecru felt. Stitch in place.

9. Using scallop-edged scissors, trim around edges of green felt.

10. Appliqué felt shapes to green felt. Position the 2" and 3½" dk. red felt ⅛"-wide strips and the large flowers in place as shown in Placement Diagram below.

Placement Diagram

11. Invisibly stitch strips to felt. Refer to Stitches on pages 118–123. Using decorative Straight Stitch, stitch flowers in place with two strands of black embroidery floss, having positioned mustard felt squares in center of each large flower while embroidering. Using Feather Stitch, stitch lt. green leaves in place with two strands of black embroidery floss. Using Buttonhole Stitch, stitch crescent shapes in place with two strands of gold embroidery floss as shown in Placement Diagram.

12. Using fanned-out Straight Stitch, stitch circles in place with two strands of gold embroidery floss as shown in Placement Diagram.

13. Position green felt piece on ecru felt ½" up from bottom edge and centered between sides. Machine-stitch in place along sides and bottom edge as shown in Placement Diagram.

14. Beginning and ending at ends of vertical ⅛" strips and using marking pencil, mark green felt at 1½" intervals. Machine-stitch on marked lines through all layers.

*P*opular for appliqué work and crazy-quilting, as well as other needlework arts, echo quilting is a technique employing multiple lines of stitches, often in several colors of thread. They follow the outline of a shape, thus the stitches "echo" either the appliquéd shape or the shape of the piece being worked, as in a handbag for example.

MATERIALS

Buttons: ⅝", *assorted antique brass (5)*; ¼", *pearl (19)*

Buttons with shanks: ¼", *dark (10)*

Cotton fabric: *white (1 yd)*

Crocheted edging with beads: *1"-wide (1 yd)*

Crocheted lace corner

Crocheted trim: *taupe, 3" x 4" for right heart*

Crystal faceted beads: *⅝"-long (6); 1"-long*

Decorative edge from ecru linen towel or pillowcase

Embroidery floss: *taupe*

Embroidered linen scrap: *white*

Flannel *(½ yd)*

Jewelry, button, vintage flower, and handkerchief *for embellishments*

Lace trims: *1"-wide (1 yd) for handle; 1¼"-wide, cream (½ yd)*

Linens: *ecru (¼ yd); cream (¼ yd); off-white (scraps); tan (scraps)*

Pearl beads

Pearl-beaded trim: *⅛"-wide (1¼ yds)*

Ready-made muslin cord *(2¼ yds)*

Seed beads: *11/0, white (1 package)*

Silk ribbon: *4mm-wide, ivory (18")*

Tape-lace pieces: *2½"-square, cream (2)*

Threads: *cream; white*

TOOLS

Beading needle

Dressmaker's pen

Embroidery needle: *size 3*

Fabric scissors

Hand-sewing needle

Iron/ironing board

Sewing machine

Straight pins

Tape measure

Tracing paper

Note: Project patterns, templates, and diagrams are shown on pages 62–66. Refer to Transferring on page 124.

1. Cut the following pieces from cotton fabric:
   one 16" x 27" and two 5½" squares for fan blocks
   one 7½" x 11½" for tulip block
   one 1¾" x 15½" for band above heart
   two 2¼" x 15½" for top band
   one 7¼" x 15½" for bottom block
   three of Template B

2. Cut 2¼" x 15½" piece from decorative edge of ecru linen towel or pillowcase.

3. Cut the following from ecru linen fabric:
   three of Template A
   ten of Fan Pattern
   two of Tulip Pattern
   two of Large Leaf Pattern
   two of Small Leaf Pattern
   two of 4½" x 5" Heart Pattern
   one of 4½" x 5" piece with embroidered design for center heart.

4. Cut the following pieces from cream linen fabric:
   two 1½" x 5½" for above fan
   three 1½" x 11½" for strips between tulips and fans
   one 1½" x 7½" for above tulip
   two of Template C
   two of Stem Pattern

5. Cut 16" x 27" piece from flannel.

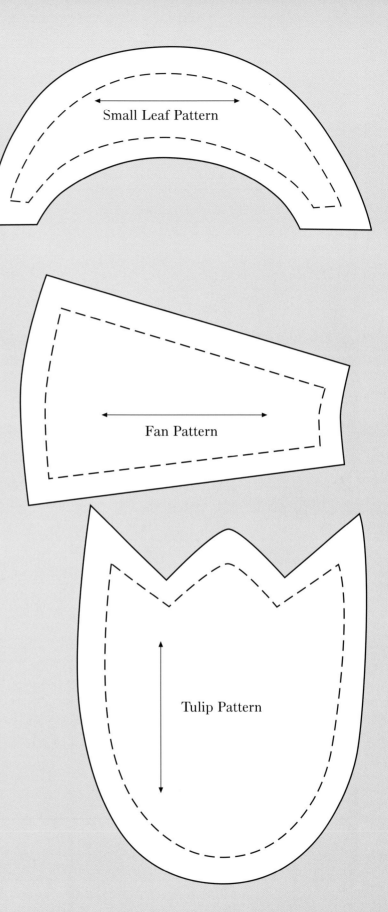

Small Leaf Pattern

Fan Pattern

Tulip Pattern

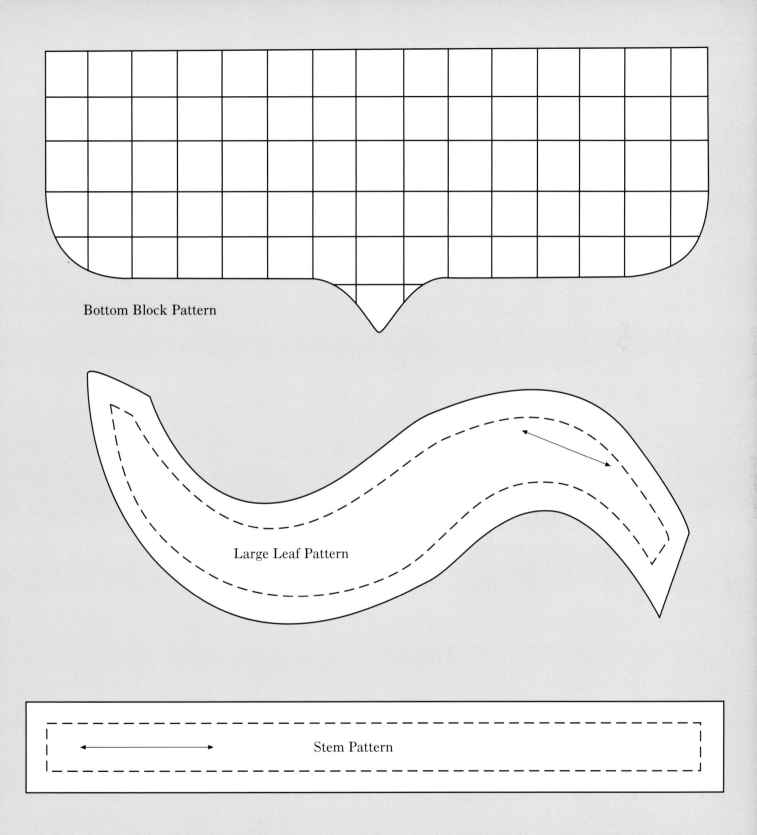

Bottom Block Pattern

Large Leaf Pattern

Stem Pattern

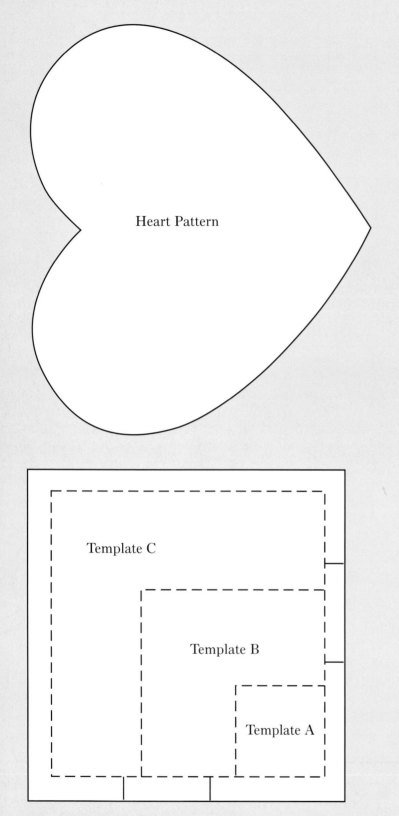

Heart Pattern

Template C

Template B

Template A

Heart & Tulip Bag Template

6. Piece Fan blocks.

a. Machine-stitch together five ecru fan pieces for upper block. Pin assembled fan to one 5½" square, matching straight outside edges. Pin excess into tucks at two inside seams as shown in Diagram A below. *Note: Tucks will be ¼" deep at outside arc.*

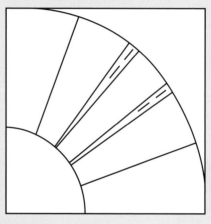

Diagram A

b. Repeat to make lower block, making two outside seams into tucks. Appliqué fans. Refer to Stitches on pages 118–123. Using Buttonhole Stitch, secure tucks with two strands of embroidery floss, tapering stitches toward inside edge.

7. Piece center section.

a. Join fan blocks with one cream 1½" x 5½" strip. Join fan block set to white 7½" x 11½" piece, using three cream 1½" x 11½" strips as shown in Diagram B on opposite page.

b. Machine-stitch together three ecru As with cream 1½" x 7½" and cream 1½" x 5½". Stitch strip to center section. Join one white 2¼" x 15½" strip to top edge of center as shown in Diagram B.

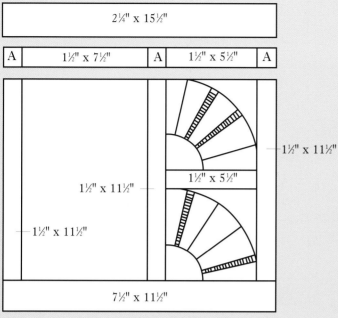

Diagram B

8. Appliqué tulips.

a. Mark placement for stems. Appliqué small leaves, then stems, large leaves overlapping stems, and flowers as shown in Diagram C below.

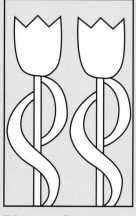

Diagram C

b. Using Feather Stitch, stitch leaves of left tulip with two strands of floss.

c. Pin decorative edge over 2¼" x 15½" white cotton strip. Machine-stitch to bottom edge of center section, securing both pieces in seam.

9. Complete lower section.

a. Machine-stitch five cream Cs together. Appliqué three white Bs on point over top of three Cs as shown in Diagram D below. Appliqué lace doilies to remaining Cs.

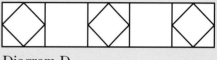

Diagram D

b. Pin decorative cream trim over white 1¾" x 15½" strip. Machine-stitch to bottom edge of pointed strip, securing both pieces in seam.

c. Trace Bottom Block Pattern on page 63 onto lower edge of white 7¼" x 15½" piece. Trace hearts on this piece for placement guide.

d. Cut ¼" outside pen line of bottom panel. Carefully cut ¼" inside each marked edge of hearts. Pin ecru 4½" x 5" pieces behind left and right hearts. Pin embroidered 4½" x 5" piece behind center heart. Clip curves. Fold seam allowance under and appliqué as shown in Diagram E at right.

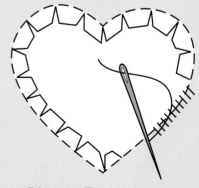

Diagram E

e. Using Buttonhole Stitch, stitch edges of hearts with one strand of floss. Join lower section to strips, then join to center section, allowing decorative edge of linen to remain loose.

10. Mark quilting lines.

a. Mark three parallel lines ½" apart on top white strip of fabric. Also mark placement for button.

11. Complete.

a. Cut ¼" outside pen line from bottom edge. Hand-stitch cord to right side of all edges of wallhanging with raw edges matching.

12. Layer purse.

a. Layer backing, wrong side up, flannel, and top. Baste-stitch through all layers. Quilt on quilting lines and close to all seam lines with white thread. Echo-quilt the tulips in rows ⅛" apart as explained on page 60. Trim backing and filler to match top. Fold seam allowances of top, flannel, and backing to inside. Slip-stitch.

13. Embellish purse.

a. Sew ¼" pearl buttons on quilting lines of upper block as shown in Heart & Tulip Bag Diagram.

b. Sew four ¼" dark buttons with shanks between pearl buttons. Sew six ¼" dark buttons with shanks evenly spaced to band above hearts. Sew six crystal faceted beads to stem of right tulip.

c. Hand-stitch pearl-beaded trim to inside circle and plain seams of each fan block. *Note: To attach one length of trim, cut length 4" longer than amount that will show. Remove 2" of pearls at one end and secure empty thread at back of quilt; repeat at opposite end.*

Heart & Tulip Bag Diagram

d. Sew five brass buttons and four pearl buttons to the band between the center and lower sections.

e. Accent embroidered designs of center heart and cream trim with small pearl beads. Tack crocheted trim to right heart. Embellish with jewelry and handkerchief as desired.

14. Hand-stitch crocheted edging with beads around bottom and side edges, beginning and ending trim at top pieced row.

15. Cut two 17½" x 19" pieces from tan linen. Fold one piece in half, aligning 17½" edges. Machine-stitch along sides, taking a ½" seam allowance. Press seam allowance open. Repeat with second piece, leaving 3" opening along one side seam. Press seam allowances open.

16. Slip second piece over first piece, with right sides facing, aligning side seams. Machine-stitch along top edge, taking a ½" seam allowance. Edge-press seam, then turn right side out though side seam opening. Press flat.

17. Place wraparound quilted piece on work surface with right side down. Place tan "pocket" onto wrong side of quilt 5½" up from bottom edge. Fold bottom edge of quilt up to form "pocket." Pin pocket in place. Hand-stitch side edges of quilt "pocket" front and back, without stitching through all layers. Tack folded-up quilt piece to pocket front along center top edge, forming three pocket openings altogether. Do not tack top edge of pocket to quilt.

18. Embellish project bag front with buttons, jewelry, vintage flower, silk ribbon, and old handkerchief. Add lace handle.

Vintage Needlework

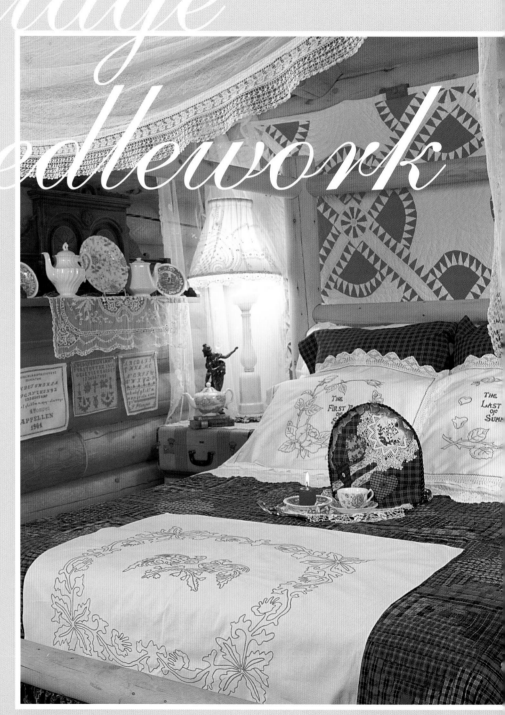

The nostalgia we feel for days gone by embraces the spirit of love that went into hours of beautiful needlework performed with such precision that handwork items took on a life of their own. It survives in the vintage embroidery, crocheted edgings, cutwork and appliqués we enjoy today. Often it is the combination of needle techniques into one item to wear or to decorate the home that holds a special significance for the piece and its maker. Needle artists of their day took pride in every embroidery, crochet, tatting, knitting, and stitching technique

During our great grandmothers' day, dry-goods shops and mail-order catalogs were treasured sources of cottons, linens, silks, velvets, and the necessary threads and trims for needlework. Buttons, lace, fringe, beads of jet as well as black and red coral, seed pearls, and ribbon were sought after to make "pretties" for the home or to wear. In rural areas, trips to a dry-goods store were infrequent, so using every scrap of fabric and needle technique that had been mastered to create practical and intricately beautiful items was an art form. Those who did so at an appreciated level of excellence were highly esteemed in their communities. Where they passed down their skills to their children, we are the benefactors. The revival of needle arts as a personal pastime that offers relief from stress also brings us creative pleasure and comfort.

they learned. Their unique handwork might include Redwork or Turkish embroidery on fine linen, or a lace-edged tablecloth with perhaps appliquéd flowers or cutwork as a personal signature that became recognized among their circle of friends and family. Baby and wedding gifts were wondrous creations for loved ones. Using samplers of outline and satin-stitched alphabets, mothers challenged daughters to learn essential stitches and decorative French knots to become expert needleworkers.

PICTURE-PERFECT REDWORK

*T*he story of Redwork begins with the Turkish red dye that was used to dye thread for Turkish carpets. The dye was made from the madder plant, oil, and other secret ingredients.

The dye eventually made its way to Europe where it was used to dye cotton thread. The Turkish red thread was popular because it was colorfast and would hold up well under repeated washings and lying out in the sun. In Europe, it was used primarily for embroidery on linens.

When the German-speaking immigrants came to our country and settled in Pennsylvania and Ohio, they brought their love of Redwork with them. Their use of the thread resulted in it being imported from Europe.

MATERIALS

Copy machine
Frame
Stranded embroidery floss: *red*
White linen: *12"-square*

TOOLS

Copy machine
Embroidery hoop
Embroidery needle: *size 3*
Iron/ironing board
Light-box
Permanent-ink gel pen: *red*
Press cloth
Small fabric scissors
Tracing paper

INSTRUCTIONS

1. Enlarge desired Redwork Transfer Pattern on page 72 200%. Refer to Transferring on page 124. Using light-box and gel pen, trace pattern onto linen fabric. Using iron, heat-set ink after design has been traced.

2. Using embroidery hoop, embroider design with a combination of basic stitches and one or two strands of floss, depending upon area being stitched. Refer to Stitches on pages 118–123. Outline shapes, using either Outline Stitch or Backstitch. Using Satin Stitch, fill in larger spaces. Using Straight Stitch, add tiny details. Create texture with French Knot Stitches.

3. Once embroidery is completed, and using press cloth, press work from wrong side.

Redwork Transfer Pattern #1

Redwork Transfer Pattern #2

By the late 1800s and early 1900s, Turkish Redwork had spread ethnically and geographically in America and was very popular. By that time, it was being used in summer coverlets and spreads as well as linens. Patterns transferred onto muslin squares could be obtained for one penny from the dry-goods stores and catalogs, resulting in the term "penny squares." Many patterns were hand-drawn or traced from magazines and newspapers. Later, a variety of patterns appeared in catalogs and could be ordered.

The popularity of Redwork was on the wane by the 1920s as cotton embroidery thread became readily available in other colors.

Redwork Transfer Pattern #3

*I*n monogramming etiquette, prominence is always given to the letter of the surname. The surname initial is sized larger and placed in the center. It is flanked by smaller letters for first and middle names, or a couple's first initials. If the letters are all the same size, they should follow the regular rotation of the first, middle (or maiden), and last names. When the letters in a monogram entwine, determine which of the cross-lines should be brought forward to emphasize the surname initial.

Monogram Embroidery

The simplest letters can be enhanced with auxiliary stitches and finely executed embroidery designs. It will be necessary to use a round Swiss or tambour frame for small work, and a piece of very strong fabric, such as drill sewn to the frame and stretched very tightly for large pieces. A square opening is cut in the center, large enough for the entire design to be worked. The work is then placed beneath this opening, made straight by the threads of the fabric, fastened with pins, and tacked into position with small stitches. The rest of the fabric is folded out of the way. Once the fabric to be monogrammed is secured for embroidering, it can be enriched with ornamental scrolls, and a variety of stitches to break each letter into light and shadow.

MATERIALS

Corded embroidery floss: *dusty aqua for sprays and flourish*

Edge or corners of vintage embroidered piece

Frame

Linen: *44"–54" wide, lt. olive green (¾ yd); natural, 12" x 15"*

Silk ribbons: *⅛"-wide, lt. olive (½ yd); ¼"-wide, ivory, (½ yd); 4mm-wide, taupe (½ yd)*

Standard binder with 2½"-wide spine

Stranded embroidery flosses: *cotton, pale aqua for spray stems and flourish detail; rayon, pale green for lettering*

Vintage lace trim: *½"-wide (½ yd)*

TOOLS

Embroidery hoop

Embroidery needle: *size 3*

Iron/ironing board

Light-box

Permanent-ink gel pen: *lt. blue or green*

Press cloth

Small fabric scissors

Straight pins

Tracing paper

INSTRUCTIONS

1. Refer to Transferring on page 124. Using light-box and gel pen, trace desired initials from Alphabet and Monogram Design on pages 75–77 onto center of linen. Using iron, heat-set ink after design has been traced.

2. Refer to Stitches on pages 118–123. Using Satin Stitch, work lettering with two strands of the rayon floss.

3. Using Stem Stitch, work stem sprays with three strands of cotton floss.

4. Using Bullion Lazy Daisy Stitch, work sprays with two strands of corded floss. *Note: The floss is wrapped two times around the needle.*

5. Using Coral Stitch, work flourish with two strands of corded floss.

6. Using Outline Stitch, work flourish detail with cotton floss. Fill flourish's open space with cotton and rayon flosses. Once embroidery is completed, using press cloth, press work from wrong side.

7. Cut fabric for binder cover. Trim monogrammed piece to 11½" x 12¾". Cut 12¾" x 15⅝" piece from lt. olive green linen for spine/back. Cut two 11½" x 12¾" pieces from lt. olive green linen for pockets. Cut 12¾" x 26¼" piece from lt. olive green linen for lining.

8. Stitch cover. Stitch spine/back piece to front, aligning 12¾" edges, taking a ½" seam allowance. Press seam allowance open. *Note: This is the outer cover.* Overlap ribbon onto lace and stitch over seam along right edge of ribbon. Press. Stitch a narrow hem along one 12¾" edge of each pocket, press. Pin opposite edge of each pocket to left and right edge of outer cover, right sides facing. Pin pockets to upper and lower edges of outer cover as well. Pin and stitch lining to outer cover/pockets, right sides facing, taking a ½" seam allowance and leaving a 4" opening along the back bottom edge. Clip bulk from corners and edge-press seam allowances open. Turn right side out through opening. Push out corners and press well, with steam and spray starch, if necessary.

9. Slip binder into cover pockets.

10. Loop ¼" ribbon and tack to the center of the light olive green ribbon, using 4mm ribbon. Using Cascade Stitch, stitch ends of 4mm ribbon.

Monogram Design

A B
C D
E F

G H I J K

Alphabet

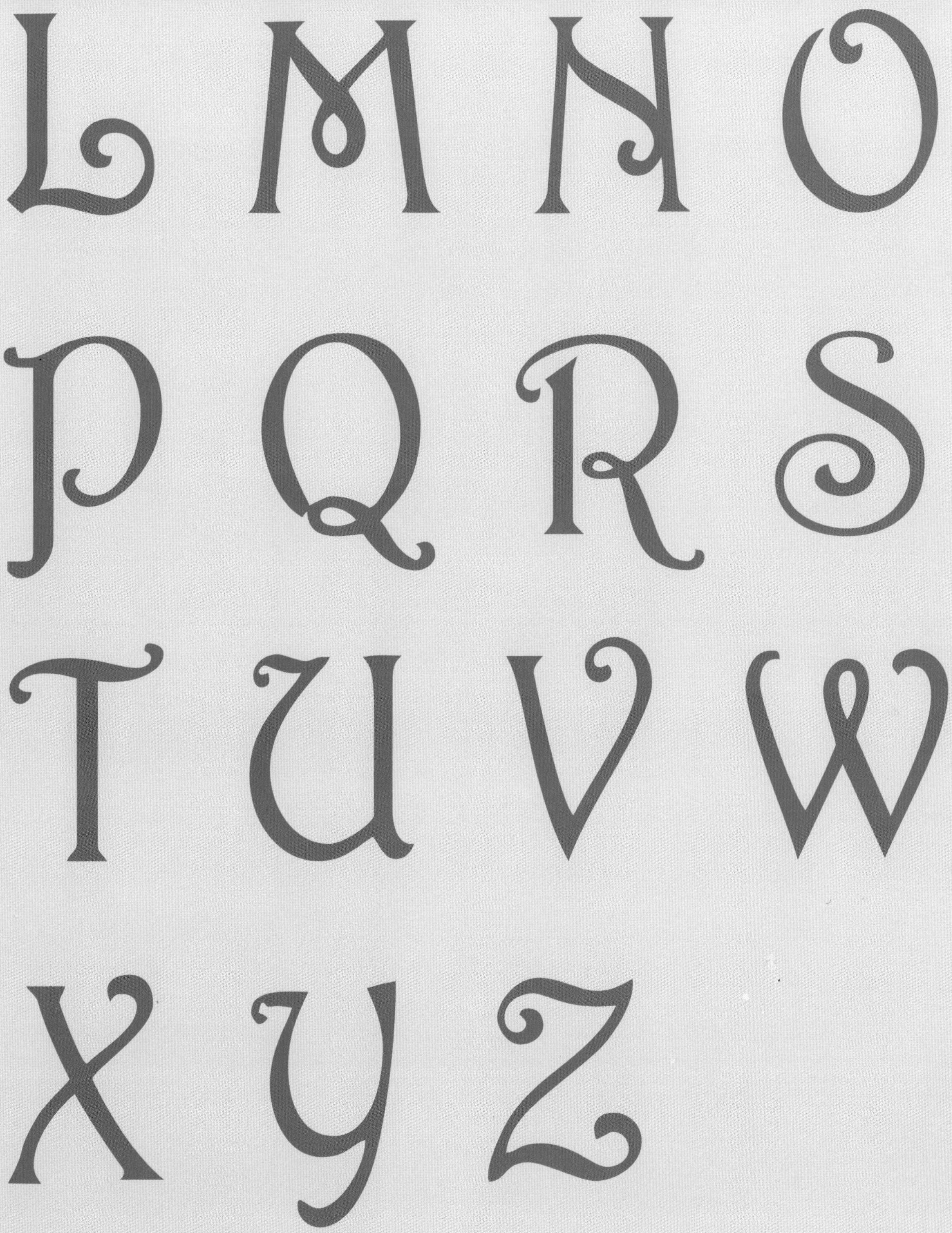

L M N O
P Q R S
T U V W
X Y Z

Alphabet

TIMELESS MANTEL CLOTH

he Coral Stitch is an effective outline stitch where curved lines or a knotted or "broken up" appearance is desired. The name coral comes from the effect of beads at intervals on a thread. It is oftentimes a stitch found in Teneriffe embroidery. It can be worked downward, or from right to left.

MATERIALS

Crochet thread: *20–30 weight*
Embroidery floss: *wheat*
Fine linen: *natural 17½" x 72"*
Matching thread
Vintage crocheted edging: *3"-wide, ecru (3 yds)*

TOOLS

Copy machine
Craft scissors
Hand-sewing needle
Iron/ironing board
Light-box
Permanent-ink gel pen: *lt. brown*
Steel crochet hook: *size 8*
Straight pins
Tape measure
Tracing paper
Transparent tape

ace the Radiance of Life

INSTRUCTIONS

1. Fold and press ends of linen under 3", pressing raw end ½" under as well. Invisibly hand-stitch in place along inner folded-under edge.

2. Finish top edge of linen with crocheted edge. Beginning at one end, single-crochet along raw edge, working needle into fabric ⅛" while crocheting. At every ten Sc, make two Dc.

3. Crochet 3"-wide edging. Whipstitch crocheted edge to bottom edge of linen cloth. Press well.

4. Enlarge Mantel Cloth Transfer Pattern at right 200%. Trim words, then tape them together, aligning bottom edges of letter and leaving 2" space between words. Fold length of words in half to find center. Fold length of linen in half to find center. Mark center with a pin at center bottom edge.

5. Refer to Transferring on page 124. Using gel pen and light-box, trace lettering onto center bottom edge of linen cloth, placing lettering 1⅛" up from bottom edge, matching center of lettering with center of linen cloth. Heat-set lettering.

6. Refer to Stitches on pages 118–123. Using Coral Stitch, embroider lettering with three strands of embroidery floss.

Embrace the Radiance of Life

Mantel Cloth Transfer Pattern

Cutwork embroidery, or cut-and-drawn work, is performed on fabric in which the warp and weft threads are of the same thickness. The open spaces formed by removing threads will always be exact and predictable in a complex design. Cutwork is generally worked in an embroidery frame to maintain its stability until the edging stitches used can secure the fabric threads from raveling. This technique is especially suited for borders.

Basics for Cutwork:

Cutwork embroidery is a form of needle-work where portions of background fabric are cut away and discarded. The cut edges are then stitched with buttonhole stitches. The simplest form of cutwork is that which contains small open areas, such as eyelets, with no connecting bars.

Fabrics for Cutwork:

Cutwork embroidery works best on linen fabric. It also can be worked on plain-weave cotton fabric, but linen fabric has a richer look and suits the elegance of cutwork. Preshrink fabrics prior to embroidery.

Flosses for Cutwork:

Cutwork has traditionally been stitched with a twisted, nondivisible mercerized cotton, such as DMC®'s brilliant cutwork and embroidery thread, size 16. This thread is currently available only in basic shades, such as white and ecru. Do not use stranded thread for cutwork embroidery. In order to add color to the cutwork embroidery, a substitute for the traditional thread is DMC's Cebelia™ crochet cotton, size 30. The Cebelia is available in 569 yd balls, which is enough thread for several projects. This thread is a three-cord crochet cotton. Use a small embroidery hoop to pull fabric taut while stitching.

VINTAGE CUTWORK TABLECLOTH

Basic Stitches for Cutwork:

The cutwork is worked using the Buttonhole Stitch, with the space being represented as a double solid line. The ridge created by the Buttonhole Stitch is always placed along the edge that will be trimmed away, whether it be an outward edge, or an inner space. For those pieces with delicate sprays, stitch stems with Stem Stitch. Using the Satin Stitch, fill open spaces.

Trimming and Finishing for Cutwork:

After having been worked, press the embroidery from the wrong side. Stiffen the fabric with one light coat of spray starch, then press again from the wrong side. Using sharp embroidery scissors, carefully trim away the excess fabric from the outer edges or inner spaces. Trim right up to the ridge created by the Buttonhole Stitch, being careful to not cut through the embroidery. When the piece has been completely trimmed, lightly spray-starch again from the wrong side, then trim away any fabric frays that remain. Lightly spray-starch once more from the wrong side. Press.

MATERIALS

Cutwork embroidery floss: *lt. blue*

Linen: *white, 16" x 24"*

TOOLS

Copy machine

Embroidery hoop

Embroidery needle: *size 3*

Iron/ironing board

Light-box

Permanent-ink gel pen: *lt. blue*

Small fabric scissors

Tracing paper

INSTRUCTIONS

1. Enlarge Embroidery Design 200% at right. Refer to Transferring on page 124. Using light-box and gel pen, trace Embroidery Design onto linen fabric.

2. Using iron, heat-set ink after design has been traced.

3. Refer to Stitches on pages 118–123. Using embroidery hoop and Buttonhole Stitch, embroider design. Using Outline Stitch, embroider small line details. Using Satin Stitch, embroider small circles.

Embroidery Design

FLORAL EMBELLISHED PILLOW

*S*ilk ribbon embroidery, particularly when it is used to make roses, flowers, and leaves, has a delicate effect worked on fine linen. In China, Japan, Australia, Europe, and the United States, it is regaining its popularity, especially when incorporated into crazy-quilting. When combined with lace and pieced fabrics in harmony with each other, as for this pillow top, the ribbon embroidery creates the lush focal point. Exquisite details of tiny buds and baby leaves extend from the mature flower blossoms and leaves in bouquet style.

MATERIALS

Floral-print fabric: *pale rose tone-on-tone (½ yd)*

Lace trim: *1¼"-wide, ecru (1 yd)*

Matching threads

Organza ribbons: *9mm-wide, tan (2 yds); 18mm-wide, celery (1½ yds); 18mm-wide, pale pink (2½ yds)*

Pillow form: *14"*

Silk ribbons: *4mm-wide, lt. avocado (1¼ yd); 4mm-wide, gold (1¼ yd); 4mm-wide, pale green (2 yds); 4mm-wide, olive (4 yds); 4mm-wide, purple (1 yd); 4mm-wide, dk. purple (1 yd); 7mm-wide, lt. gold (2½ yds); 7mm-wide, fern green (1¼ yds); 13mm-wide, mauve/pink (¾ yd); 13mm-wide, dusty purple (¾ yd)*

Ticking fabric: *lt. rose striped (¼ yd)*

Variegated ribbons: *7mm-wide, ivory (2 yds); 7mm-wide, plum (1 yd); 7mm-wide, terra-cotta (1¼ yds); 13mm-wide, lt. lavender (1¼ yds); 13mm-wide, olive (1¼ yds); 13mm-wide, bubblegum pink (2 yds); 13mm-wide, terra-cotta (1¼ yds)*

TOOLS

Chenille needle: *size 20*

Darning needle: *large-eyed*

Embroidery needle: *size 3*

Fabric scissors

Hand-sewing needle

Iron/ironing board

Light-box

Pencil

Sewing machine

Straight pins

Tape measure

Tracing paper

1. Cut 10" square from floral fabric for front.

2. Center and trace 8" square onto wrong side of cut piece. Baste-stitch on traced line.

3. Refer to Transferring on page 124. Using light-box and pencil, lightly trace Floral Embellished Pillow Transfer Pattern on opposite page onto center right side of cut piece.

4. Refer to Stitches on pages 118–123. Embroider design, following Floral Embellished Pillow Stitch Guides below and on pages 88–89.

5. Once worked, trim embroidered fabric ½" past baste-stitching. Cut four 6½" x 9" pieces from pale rose striped fabric. Machine-stitch each piece to opposite side of embroidered fabric, right sides together, taking ½" seam allowance. Catch piece from previous sides while stitching. Press seams toward striped fabric. Machine-stitch lace trim over print/stripe seams. Trim to 15" square.

6. Cut two 9½" x 15" pieces from floral fabric for pillow back. Cut 2"-wide bias strips from floral fabric for total of 64". Stitch ½"-deep hem along one 15" side on each pillow back.

7. With wrong sides together, overlap and pin pillow backs to pillow front.

8. Stitch bias pieces together to form one long piece. Press seams open. Beginning near left-bottom corner, stitch bias to pillow edge, right sides together, working from pillow front. Press seam toward bias.

9. From pillow back, turn raw edge of bias under ½". Fold bias over to enclose seam. Pin to hold. Machine or hand-stitch in place. Press. Insert pillow form through back opening. Stitch opening closed.

Floral Embellished Pillow Stitch Guide

Description	Ribbon	Stitch
1. Rosebud Stem	4mm olive	Stem Stitch
2. Fern Stems Daisy Bud Stems	4mm lt. green	Stem Stitch
3. Dahlia, row 4 Stitch twelve petals along row 4 circle.	13mm bubblegum pink	Pointed Petal Stitch
4. Dahlia Buds		Crossover Lazy Daisy Stitch
5. Dahlia, row 3 Stitch twelve petals along row 3 circle.	18mm pale pink	Pointed Petal Stitch
6. Dahlia, row 2 Stitch twelve petals along row 2 circle.	13mm terra-cotta	Pointed Petal Stitch
7. Dahlia, row 1 Stitch twelve petals along row 1 circle.	18mm pale pink	Pointed Petal Stitch
8. Dahlia Center Cluster lt. gold and ivory stitches to fill Dahlia Center.	7mm lt. gold 7mm ivory	Ruffled Ribbon Stitch

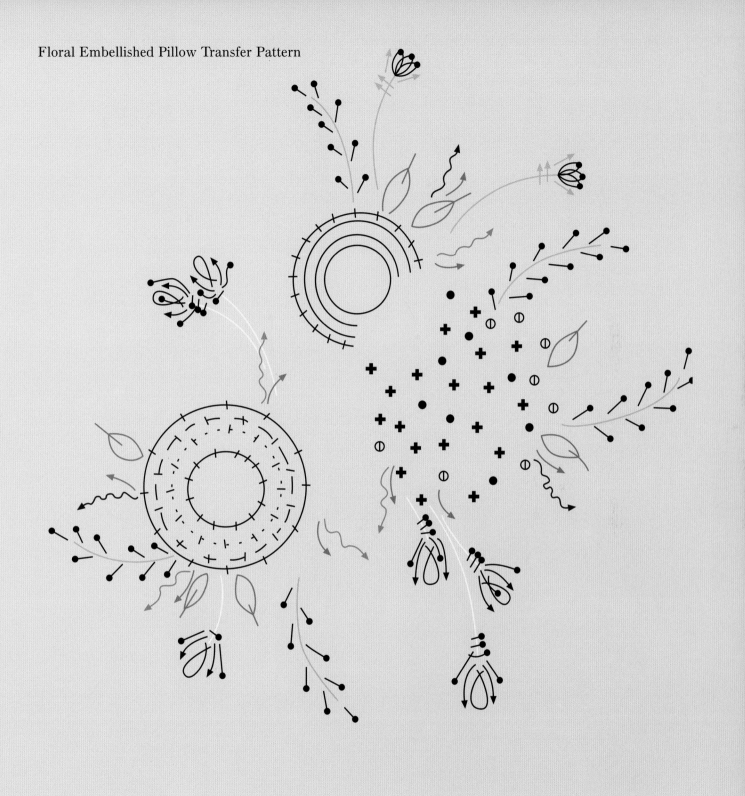

9. Dahlia Buds	7mm terra-cotta	Ribbon Stitch

Place stitches to enclose Crossover Lazy Daisy Stitches from Step 4 on page 86.

10. Daisy, Daisy Buds	7mm lt. gold	Knotted and Looped Ribbon Stitch

Position knot ¾" from entry point on ribbon. Space stitches ⅛" apart along row 4. Stitch three Knotted and Looped Ribbon Stitches for each bud.

11. Daisy, row 3	9mm tan	Knotted and Looped Ribbon Stitch

Place stitches ⅛" apart along row 3 circle.

12. Daisy, row 2	7mm ivory	Knotted and Looped Ribbon Stitch

Place stitches ⅛" apart along row 2 circle.

13. Daisy, row 1	9mm tan	Knotted and Looped Ribbon Stitch

Place stitches ⅛" apart along row 1 circle.

14. Daisy Center	4mm gold	Ruffled Ribbon Stitch

Fill daisy center.

15. Hydrangea	13mm lt. lavender	Loop Stitch
16. Hydrangea	4mm lt. avocado	Colonial Knot Stitch

Tack center above loops.

17. Hydrangea	13mm mauve/pink	Loop Stitch
18. Hydrangea	13mm dusty purple	Loop Stitch
19. Hydrangea	4mm olive	Colonial Knot Stitch

Tack center of loops from Steps 17 & 18 above.

20. Dahlia Stamens, Fern Leaves	4mm olive	Ribbon Stitch

Place stitches to enclose dahlia buds. Make 1–3 Ribbon Stitches at base of buds to cinch stitches. Stitch Ribbon Stitches along fern stems.

21. Daisy Stamens	4mm lt. green	Ribbon Stitch

Stitch as for dahlia buds, Step 20 above.

22. Leaves	13mm olive	Bullion Lazy Daisy Stitch
23. Leaves	18mm hunter green	Ribbon Stitch
24. Lavender	7mm plum	Ruffled Ribbon Stitch
25. Lavender	4mm purple 4mm dk. purple	Ruffled Ribbon Stitch

Thread together in needle and work as one.

26. Leaves	7mm fern green	Ribbon Stitch

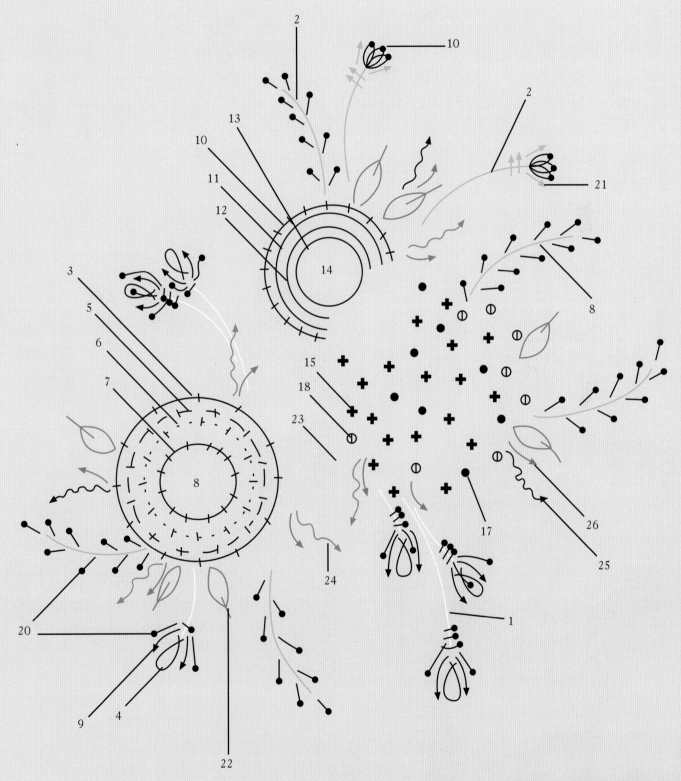

RIBBONWORK BOUQUET

overed boxes have myriad uses in the bedroom, bath, and as gifts. Small boxes, particularly handmade ones, are the essence of well-kept secrets. They can be practical for holding buttons, coins, threads, hair clips, and lipsticks, and sensory delights when stuffed to their brims with fragrant, dried rose petals or lavender blossoms. Adding a personal phrase in calligraphy makes the box an even more meaningful keepsake for self or a loved one.

MATERIALS

Chenille: *olive green (½ yd) for bow*

Cotton-covered wire: *32mm-wide (¼ yd) for gathered rosebud spray stems*

Crocheted lace scrap: *1"-wide*

Lace appliqué: *1" round*

Pearl/seed-beaded piece

Print fabric: *pale gold tone-on-tone (¼ yd)*

Round box: *5" dia., or vintage box of any size*

Satin ribbon: *1"-wide, bright coral (4") for fuchsia*

Sheer embroidered appliqué: *2"–4"*

Sheer or lightweight fabrics, *1½"-wide strips: coral for gathered rosebud sprays; ivory for dahlia outer petals; pale peach for dahlia center, single-petal rose; satiny peach for gathered rose; dk. peach for peach blossoms; pale green for leaves*

Silk ribbons, *7mm-wide: apricot for rosettes (½ yd); lt. green for covering gathered rosebud spray stems (2 yds)*

Tatted lace scrap: *¼"-wide*

TOOLS

Computer/image-editing program/printer

Deckle-edged scissors

Disposable paint roller: *3"-wide*

Fabric scissors

Flat pressing surface (such as a piece of particle board)

Florist tape

Hand-sewing needle

Ink jet transfer paper

Iron/ironing board

Phrases or poems of your choice

Press cloth

Straight pins

Tacky glue

Tracing paper

INSTRUCTIONS

1. Photocopy Box Phrase on page 95 backwards onto tracing paper or, using computer, create and print any phrase backwards onto tracing paper. Refer to Transferring on page 124. Transfer phrase onto fabric.

2. Using deckle-edged scissors, trim phrase from the tracing paper, leaving ⅛" border all around.

3. Cut pale gold fabric to cover lid top, lid sides, and box sides. For box and lid sides, press under long edges of pale gold fabric strips, before adhering them to surface. Utilizing 3" disposable roller to apply tacky glue, adhere fabric to lid.

4. Place pressing surface on a work surface and heat iron (no steam). Place a press cloth over pressing surface. Place box side fabric right side up over press cloth.

5. Position image face down on fabric. Apply hot, dry iron with firm pressure for approximately one minute, moving iron in a slow circular motion so entire phrase is pressed firmly for the same length of time. For a long phrase, cut paper in half and apply the phrase to the fabric in two pieces.

6. Allow fabric to cool for a second, then peel away backer paper in a smooth movement. Do not iron directly on transferred image. Press under long edges of box side as in Step 3. *Note: If the phrase has been applied to an item to be washed, leave the finished item for at least 24 hours before washing, using, or wearing.*

7. Make dahlia from ivory and pale peach fabrics.

a. Press ivory fabric in half, matching long edges.

b. Cut thirteen 2" pieces from folded ribbon.

c. Press folds with iron for crisp edges. Pin folds in place. See (1) at right.

d. Gather-stitch all petals together in a chain, stitching ¼" above raw edges. See (2) at right. Tightly pull to gather, then secure thread. Join last petal to first. Trim raw edges ⅛" below stitches.

e. Completed outer petal layer of dahlia. See (3) at right.

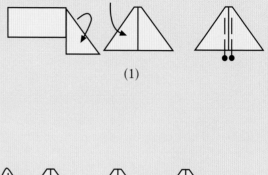

(1)

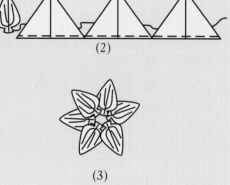

(2)

(3)

f. For lace ruffle at center of dahlia, fold 5" piece of ½"-wide lace in half, matching raw edges. Glue narrow seam. Gather-stitch along bottom edge. Pull gathers and secure thread. Glue lace ruffle onto center of dahlia. For pale peach ruffle above lace ruffle, cut 1½"-wide piece of pale peach fabric into one 7" length. Press in half, matching long edges. Fold in half, matching short edges. Stitch narrow seam. Gather-stitch along bottom edges ¼" up from raw edges. Pull gather tightly and secure thread. Trim raw edges to ⅛" below stitching. Glue pale peach ruffle to center of dahlia above lace ruffle. Glue center button to center of dahlia.

8. Make folded leaf from pale green fabric.

a. Press 15" strip in half, matching long edges. Cut into three 5" pieces.

b. Fold ends forward diagonally. See (1) below.

c. Gather-stitch across bottom edge of folds. See (2) below. Tightly pull gather and secure thread.

d. Completed folded leaf. See (3) below.

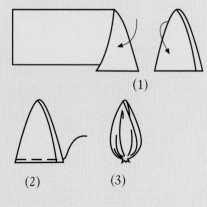

9. Make fuchsia from satin ribbon.

a. Fold length of ribbon in half and crease. Turn down one raw edge of ribbon ¼". Fold remaining raw edge of ribbon back so it overlaps center crease ¼". Fold turned-under edge of ribbon back to meet center crease. See (1) below. Pin to hold.

b. Knot 6" length of ribbon. Pull through seam from back to front for fuchsia stem. Mark diamond shape on fuchsia. Hand-gather-stitch on diamond. Tightly pull gather and secure thread. See (2) below.

c. Completed fuchsia. See (3) below.

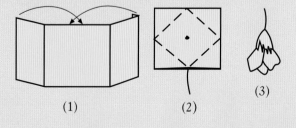

10. Make gathered rose from peach fabric.

a. Press 15" strip in half, matching long edges.

b. Fold length of fabric down at right angle, creating a post to hold onto. See (1) below.

c. Fold folded end in half. Stitch in place securely. See (2) below.

d. Gather-stitch along bottom edge of remaining length of fabric. See (3) below. Tightly pull to gather, then wrap gathered section around folded center. Stitch in place to secure.

e. Completed gathered rose. See (4) below.

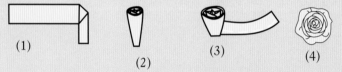

(1) (2) (3) (4)

11. Make gathered rosebud spray from coral fabric.

a. Press 39" strip in half, matching long edges. Cut into thirteen 3" lengths.

b. Fold fabric. See (1) below.

c. Fold again. See (2) below.

d. Roll folded end and secure at bottom of roll. Gather-stitch opposite end. See (3) below.

e. Tightly pull gather to form petal, then secure thread. Wrap gathered petal around center roll to form bud. See (4) below.

f. Completed gathered rosebud. See (5) below.

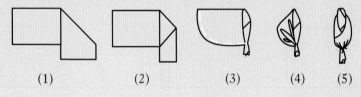

(1) (2) (3) (4) (5)

g. For spray, fold 6" length of lightweight wire in half. Stitch gathered rosebuds onto wire, spacing rosebuds ¼" apart. Wrap wire with florist tape to hide raw edges. Repeat for a second spray of five gathered rosebuds and a third spray of three gathered rosebuds.

12. Make three peach blossoms from dk. peach fabric.

a. Press 25" piece in half, matching long edges.

b. Enlarge Circle Pattern 200%. Beginning ¼" from edge, trace five half circles on fabric. Trim fabric ¼" past last half circle. Gather-stitch all half-circles together in a chain, stitching above straight edges, creating petals. See (1) below.

c. Tightly gather and secure thread. See (2) below. Join last petal to first and secure thread.

d. Completed peach blossom. See (3) below.

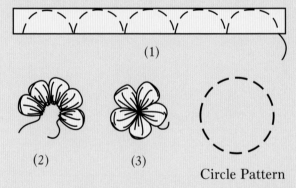

(1)

(2) (3) Circle Pattern

13. Make rosette from apricot silk ribbon, following Step 11a–f at left for gathered rosebud.

14. Make single-petal rose from pale peach fabric.

a. Press 22" strip in half, matching long edges.

b. Beginning with fabric end facing downward, fold ribbon diagonally and forward and back so fold is ⅜" deep.

c. Fold fabric diagonally forward and back, as for first fold. Pin bottom folded edge for better control.

d. After ten folds have been pinned, gather-stitch along bottom edge. Remove pins after stitching. See (1) below.

e. Fold, pin, and stitch another ten petals. If thread appears to be running short, pull thread to gather fabric.

f. Continue until entire length of fabric has been stitched into mountain folds. Tightly gather and secure thread. Straighten folds so all are facing same direction.

g. Beginning at one end, roll folds into rose. Secure on underside as needed to keep rolls in place.

h. Completed single-petal rose. See (2) below.

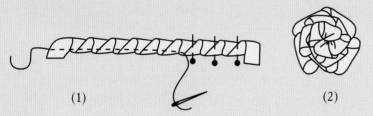

(1)   (2)

15. Arrange all flowers, lace, and beaded pieces on box top. Glue in place.

Many are proficiently engaged in doing some variety of much admired fancywork...

Box Phrase

FLORAL ACCENT BOX

*E*very pretty box is beautiful if crafted well, but a floral accent box can become a focal point to enjoy on a foyer or boudoir table. The colors of ribbon roses and other blossoms can be keyed to a gift recipient's personal taste or to the pastels of a designated room's wall coverings, upholstery, or other furnishings. The three-dimensional qualities of a box embellished with ribbon roses are as exciting to enjoy now as when such boxes were given as gifts during Victorian times. The array of materials, techniques, and box shapes available to work with today makes an overall design as unique as its creator's self-expressive ideas.

MATERIALS

Crescent board: *7" x 30"*

Embroidery flosses: *lt. green; pale olive*

Fabric: *dk. purple (¼ yd)*

Gimp: *¼"-wide (1½ yds)*

Matching threads

Organza ribbons: *5mm-wide, hunter green (1¼ yds); 5mm-wide, tan (¾ yd); 9mm-wide, tan (2 yds)*

Poster board: *9" x 20"*

Quilt batting: *medium weight (¼ yd)*

Silk jacquard fabric: *ecru (¼ yd)*

Silk ribbons, 4mm-wide: *pale grass (¾ yd); forest green (1¼ yd); pale hunter green (¾ yd); olive (1¼ yds); off-white (2¼ yds); dk. peach (¾ yd); dk. purple (1 yd); grayish purple (1 yd); dk. rose (1¼ yds); dusty rose (1¼ yds)*

Variegated ribbons, 7mm-wide: *copper (1 yd); hunter green (3 yds)*

TOOLS

½" dowel or glue stick

Brown paper bag

Clean rags (2)

Craft scissors

Disposable paint roller/tray: *3"-wide*

Fabric scissors

Hand-sewing needle

Hot-glue gun/glue sticks

Inkless ballpoint pen

Ruler

Sharp pencil

Tacky glue

Tracing paper

Transfer paper

1. Using pencil, ruler, and patterns on pages 98–101, mark and cut crescent board, poster board, and batting pieces, with craft scissors.

2. Refer to Transferring on page 124. Transfer and cut fabric pieces as indicated on patterns.

3. Make certain to label each crescent board and poster board piece appropriately. Keep together with corresponding fabric pieces.

4. Place opened out brown paper bag on work surface. Have a wet rag and dry rag at easy access to keep hands clean. Pour a small amount of tacky glue into paint roller tray. Immerse roller in glue until it is covered with a thin layer of glue.

5. Laminate box pieces as explained on page 101.

a. Laminate middle lid and base with ecru jacquard fabric.

b. Lightly glue inside lid, inside bottom, four outside sides A & B, four inside sides A & B to batting. Trim batting away from crescent board, flush to crescent-board edge and beveled inward. Pad lid with two layers of batting, trimmed and beleved.

c. Snugly wrap fabric around crescent-board pieces. Be certain to trim all bulk from corners. Wrap outside sides A & B with ecru jacquard fabric pieces. Wrap

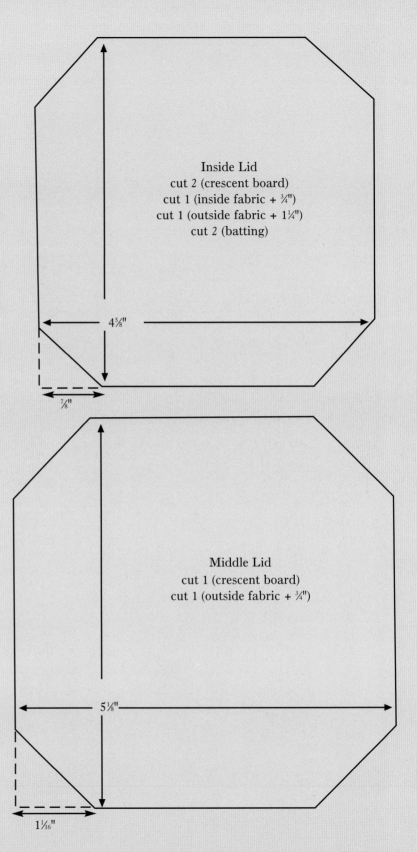

Inside Lid
cut 2 (crescent board)
cut 1 (inside fabric + ¾")
cut 1 (outside fabric + 1¼")
cut 2 (batting)

4⅝"

⅞"

Middle Lid
cut 1 (crescent board)
cut 1 (outside fabric + ¾")

5⅛"

1 1/16"

inside lid and inside bottom with dk. purple fabric. Wrap inside sides A & B with dk. purple fabric. Place outside box sides A & B on work surface, wrong side up. Carefully, roll each piece with glue stick or dowel beginning at a straight edge. Place inside box sides A & B on work surface, right side up. Carefully roll each piece with glue stick or dowel, beginning at a straight edge.

6. Assemble box bottom.

a. Hand-whipstitch outside sides A & B together with doubled matching thread. Be certain to securely and invisibly knot thread at beginning and ending of "seam."

b. Working with sides upside down, slip inside bottom into assembled outside side. Secure with a thin bead of hot glue. Work small sections at a time and hold glue until dry.

c. Glue narrow gimp over each outside seam.

d. For lid hinge, fold a 4" x 3" piece of fabric over ½" on each 3" side. Press. Fold lid hinge fabric in half, matching pressed edges. Stitch or glue pressed edges together. Glue one long edge of lid hinge fabric to wrong side top edge of an outside side A.

e. Flute while gluing 7mm variegated hunter green ribbon to one straight edge of each inside side A & B. Align and glue inside sides A & B to outside sides A & B, wrong sides together, having fluted edge as top edge.

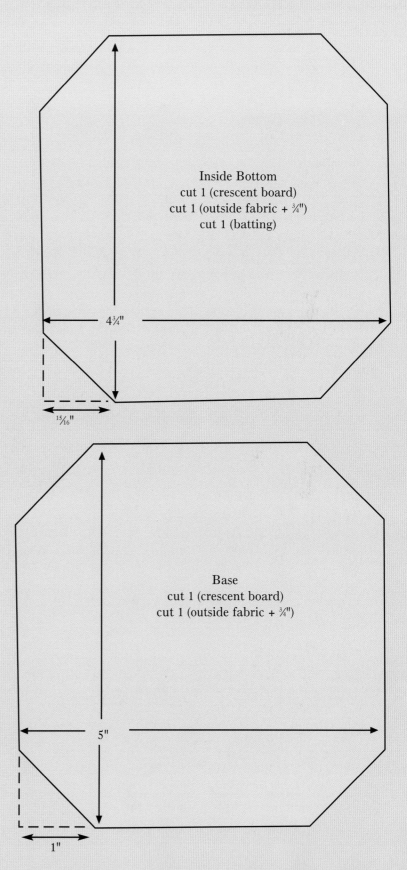

Inside Bottom
cut 1 (crescent board)
cut 1 (outside fabric + ¾")
cut 1 (batting)

4¾"

¹⁵⁄₁₆"

Base
cut 1 (crescent board)
cut 1 (outside fabric + ¾")

5"

1"

f. Glue wrong side of base to box bottom. Glue narrow gimp to bottom edge of box.

7. Trace lid shape onto wrong side of lid fabric. Baste-stitch on traced line. Using Floral Accent Box Transfer Pattern on page 101, transfer main embroidery elements to right side of fabric within baste stitching. Embroider, following Floral Accent Box Stitch Guides on pages 102–103.

8. Assemble lid and finish box. Wrap padded lid with embroidered fabric.

a. Measure and mark ⅛" from top edge of box inside onto lid hinge fabric. Glue edge of wrong side of inside lid to mark on lid hinge fabric. Close inside lid over box bottom to make certain hinge is not binding. Glue right side of middle lid to wrong side of inside lid.

b. Flute as explained below while gluing 9mm tan organza ribbon to underside edge of lid. Glue lid to middle lid, wrong sides together.

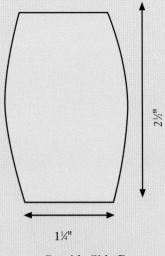

2½"

1¼"

Outside Side B
cut 4 (poster board)
cut 4 (outside fabric + ¾")
cut 4 (batting)

FLUTING

1. Glue one ribbon end to fabric or under-side of cardboard. Loop ¼" deep and glue, keeping ribbon angled.

2. Repeat, making a series of even, angled loops.

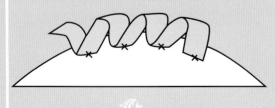

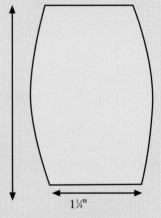

2⁵⁄₁₆"

1¼"

Inside Side B
cut 4 (poster board)
cut 4 (inside fabric + ¾")
cut 4 (batting)

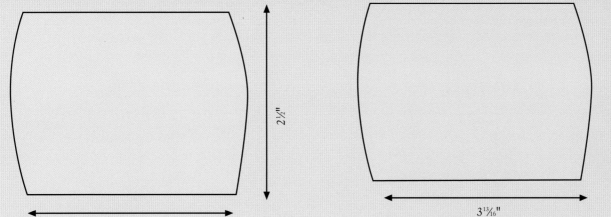

$2\frac{1}{2}''$

$3\frac{13}{16}''$

Outside Side A
cut 4 (poster board)
cut 4 (outside fabric + ¾")
cut 4 (batting)

$2\frac{5}{16}''$

$3\frac{13}{16}''$

Inside Side A
cut 4 (poster board)
cut 4 (inside fabric + ¾")
cut 4 (batting)

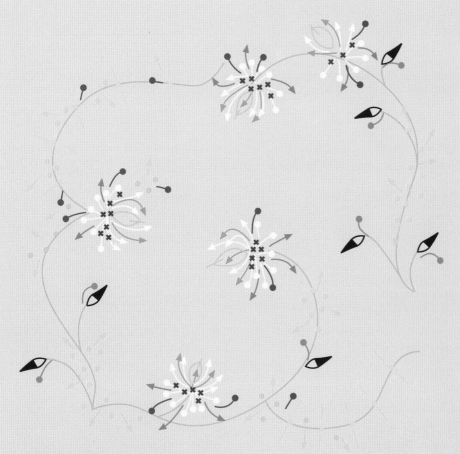

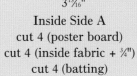

LAMINATE

1. Roll a thin layer and thorough layer of tacky glue onto crescent board or poster board. Center and place glued side onto wrong side of corresponding fabric. Smooth out fabric completely.

2. Trim off all bulk from corners. Glue and wrap extending fabric around to underside.

Floral Accent Box Transfer Pattern

Floral Accent Box Stitch Guide

Description	Ribbon	Stitch
1. Stems	flosses	Stem Stitch
2. Rose Centers	7mm copper	Bullion Lazy Daisy Stitch
3. Rose Petals Layer stitches.	4mm off-white	Twisted Ribbon Stitch
4. Rose Petals Layer stitches.	4mm grayish purple	Twisted Ribbon Stitch
5. Rose Petals Layer stitches.	5mm tan	Loop Petal Stitch
6. Rose Texture	4mm dk. rose	Knotted and Looped Ribbon Stitch

Layer among sheer Loop Petal Stitches.

Description	Ribbon	Stitch
7. Bow Flower Spray	4mm pale grass	Loop Petal Stitch

One loop on each side of stem. Bottom layer for one of the bow flower sprays.

Description	Ribbon	Stitch
8. Bow Flower Spray	4mm olive	Loop Petal Stitch

One loop on each side of stem. Bottom layer for one of the bow flower sprays. This shade is bottom layer for second spray. Layer top pale grass Loop Petal Stitches from first spray.

Description	Ribbon	Stitch
9. Bow Flower Spray	4mm off-white	Loop Petal Stitch

One loop on each side of stem. Bottom layer for one of the bow flower sprays. Layer over olive Loop Petal Stitches on both sprays. Place a Ribbon Stitch over loop centers to create the bow.

Description	Ribbon	Stitch
10. Dark Buds	4mm dk. purple	Bullion Lazy Daisy Stitch
11. Blossoms	4mm dusty rose	Loop Stich

Use two strands of floss to stitch a Colonial Knot Stitch at center of each loop.

Description	Ribbon	Stitch
12. Blossoms	4mm dk. peach	Loop Stitch

Use two strands of floss to stitch a Colonial Knot Stitch at center of each loop.

Description	Ribbon	Stitch
13. Large Leaves Near roses.	7mm hunter green	Ribbon Stitch
14. Leaves	4mm forest green	Ribbon Stitch
15. Leaves Near dark buds.	4mm pale hunter green	Ribbon Stitch
16. Sheer Leaves	5mm hunter green	Ribbon Stitch

Floral Accent Box Stitch Guide

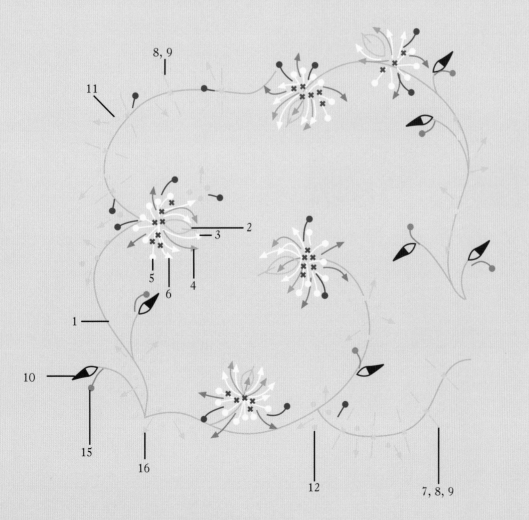

8, 9

11

2
3

5

6

4

1

10

15

16

12

7, 8, 9

LOVELY LACE TOWELS

*L*ace edging does not always need to go on the edge. Try combining lace with ribbon and laying it over the towel itself. A pattern has been provided for crochet lace. However, lace can be purchased or recycled lace can be added to new towels. Tatted, filleted, and lace doilies can be used to decorate other items.

MATERIALS

Assorted lace trims: *1"–7" wide, dk.
  ecru (¾ yd each) for bath towels;
  (½ yd each) for hand towels*

Crochet thread

Matching threads

Plush terry-cloth bath towels: *blush; tan*

Plush terry-cloth hand towels: *ecru; lt.
  olive; olive*

TOOLS

Needlepoint needle

Sewing machine

Straight pins

INSTRUCTIONS

1. Crochet edgings for towels as desired or follow suggested pattern:

a. First row: Ch 6, in 6th ch from hook make 2 dc, ch 2, and 2 dc (shell). Ch 5, turn.

b. Second row: Shell in ch-2 of shell. Ch, 5, turn.

c. Third row: Shell over shell, ch 2, skip 1 dc of shell below, dc in next dc, 3 dc in sp. Ch 1, turn.

d. Fourth row: Dc in next 4 dc, ch 2, dc in next dc, ch 2, shell over shell. Ch 5, turn.

e. Fifth row: Shell over shell, ch 2, skip 1 dc, dc in next dc, ch 2, dc in next dc, 2 dc of sp. Dc in next dc, ch 2 skip 2 dc, dc in next dc, 16 dc in ch-10 loop: ch5, tr\ at base of 1st shell made. Ch 2, turn.

f. Sixth row: Dc in 3rd ch of ch-5, n (skip 1 dc, dc in next dc, ch 5, dc in last dc) 7 times; skip 1 dc, dc in next dc, 2 dc in sp, dc in next dc, (ch 2, dc in next dc) twice; ch 2, shell over shell. Ch 5, turn.

g. Seventh and eighth rows: Shell over shell. Ch 5, turn.

h. Ninth and tenth rows: Repeat third an fourth rows.

i. Eleventh row: Shell over shell, ch 2, skip 1 dc, dc in next dc, ch 2, dc in next dc, 2 dc in sp, dc in next dc, ch 2, skip 2 dc, dc in next dc, 16 dc in ch-10 loop, ch 5, sc in 3rd sp (counting shell) on last row of last scallop. Ch 2, turn.

j. Twelfth row: Repeat sixth through eleventh rows, include for length as desired. Do not break off but work along long side as follows: *, ch 5, sc in next loop. Repeat from * across.

2. Arrange trims along bottom edges of towels. Pin in place when pleased with the arrangement. Using narrow machine-stitch, stitch trims in place.

CROCHETED EDGINGS

Beginning with a foundation row of crochet in a repeat pattern, chain stitches are created that link in regular intervals to make loops or fringes of uniform size attached to the foundation row. The edgings may be crocheted directly into the fabric they are to decorate, or may be created in lengths and then stitched by hand and needle or machine to the piece to be finished.

Historically, the finer threads and most delicate edging designs were used on lingerie or "Church Work," while the everyday linens for home and wear might be of a more coarse nature in thread weight and fineness of linen or cotton count. Edging is both beautiful and practical, for it was and is a "pretty" way to prevent the raveling of a hem.

*F*ew textures in the field of needle arts can compete with the visual and tactile appeal of fine beadwork. Whether used to enhance a hair ornament, an evening bag, an album cover, or a bed pillow. Borders and flowers are favorite themes in beadwork of the past and the present. Cross-stitch designs can be as easily worked in beads as in threads and are elegant heirlooms.

Materials

Batting

Crescent board

Cross-dyed silk dupioni fabric: *44"-wide (¼ yd)*

Cross-dyed velvet fabric: *44"-wide (¼ yd)*

Needlepoint canvas: *14-count, 9" square, ecru*

Purchased square or rectangular box: *approximately 5¼" x 6 x 1½"*

Seed beads, 11/0: *black; brown; clear; gold; gray; olive; opaque; tan; white*

Variegated embroidery floss: *olive green*

Velvet ribbon: *⅛"-wide, black*

Tools

Beading needle

Copy machine

Craft scissors

Iron/ironing board

Hot-glue gun/glue sticks

Pencil

Tacky glue

Tape measure

Tapestry needle

Floss Chart

	BD	CS
Variagated Olive Green		╲
Variagated Olive Green		╱
White	·	
Clear	⊠	
Opaque	▥	
Gold	★	
Olive	▲	
Tan	◎	
Brown	■	
Gray	▥	
Black	■	

Instructions

1. Refer to Stitches on pages 118–123. Using Continental Stitch, work leaf and rose design with beads and work the background with floss, using Floss Chart and following Beaded Keepsake Holder graph on opposite page.

2. Stitch 2"-wide dupioni fabric to sides of worked piece. Press seams toward dupioni.

3. Remove box lid, set aside for another project. Trace box opening onto crescent board. Cut out, label as Lid. Trace Lid two times, adding ⅛" all around. Cut out, label one Middle Lid, label the other Base. Trace Lid again, decrease ⅛" all around. Cut out, label as Inside Bottom. Trace Inside Bottom four times, but label each of these as Inside Lid. Glue together four Inside Lids.

4. Cover box with velvet and silk fabrics. Using tacky glue, glue velvet fabric to inside and outside of box and Middle Lid. Adhere silk dupioni to Base, Inside Lid, and Inside Bottom. Wrap raw edges to wrong sides.

5. Glue batting to Lid, trim batting flush with cardboard. Snugly wrap beaded piece around Lid. Trim fabric bulk from corners when wrapping around Lid.

6. Using hot glue, glue wrong side of Lid to right side of Middle Lid. Glue Inside Lid to Middle Lid, wrong sides facing. Glue Inside Bottom to inside of box, covering raw edges of velvet that were glued to inside of box.

7. Beginning at center of one box side, glue black velvet ribbon to bottom edge of box. Cover raw edges where velvet ends meet with another piece of velvet ribbon. Glue wrong side of Base to box bottom.

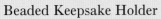

Beaded Keepsake Holder

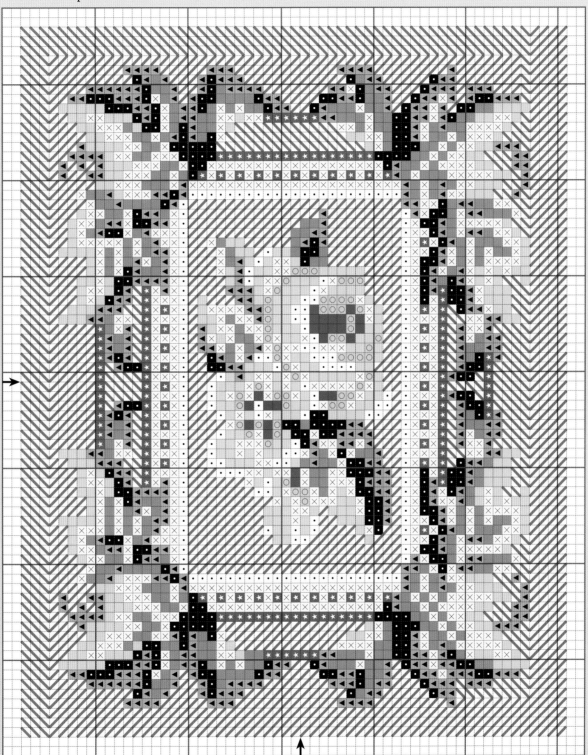

CROSS-STITCH REMEMBRANCE

*C*ross-stitch is a timeless technique. Vintage clothing and household items embellished with cross-stitch designs are still beautiful after years of use. Historically, nearly every culture known for its needle arts has employed some sort of cross-stitch pattern in enhancements for borders on hems and sleeves, curtains, religious vestments, and everyday items. Whether sophisticated in thread and fabric treatment such as white on white, shades of one color, or elaborately folk-art in style with many bright colors, cross-stitch designs add textural beauty to wall hangings, clothing, pillows, and practical household and bed linens.

MATERIALS

Belfast linen: *32 count, cream*

Embroidery flosses per DMC®
  Floss Chart

TOOLS

Embroidery needle

Fabric scissors

DMC Floss Chart

	XS	BS	FK
White	·		
746			
3047	+		
225			
224	■	⌐	
223	▣		
221	■		
3326	▪		
503	■		
501	★		
522	▽		
934	■		
407	H	⌐	
632	▨	└	●

INSTRUCTIONS

1. Stitch design on Belfast linen over two threads, following Cross-stitch Remembrance graphs on pages 111–116. *Note: Finished design size is 12¾" x 12". Cut fabric 19" x 18". Finished design sizes, using other fabrics are: Aida 11 18⅝" x 17⅞"; Aida 14 14⅞" x 13¾"; Aida 18 11⅜" x 10¾"; Hardanger 22 9¼" x 8¼".*

The antique sampler from which this design was patterned is owned by Suzanne Sarver of Ogden, Utah. She purchased the piece in 1974 from an antique dealer in Michigan.

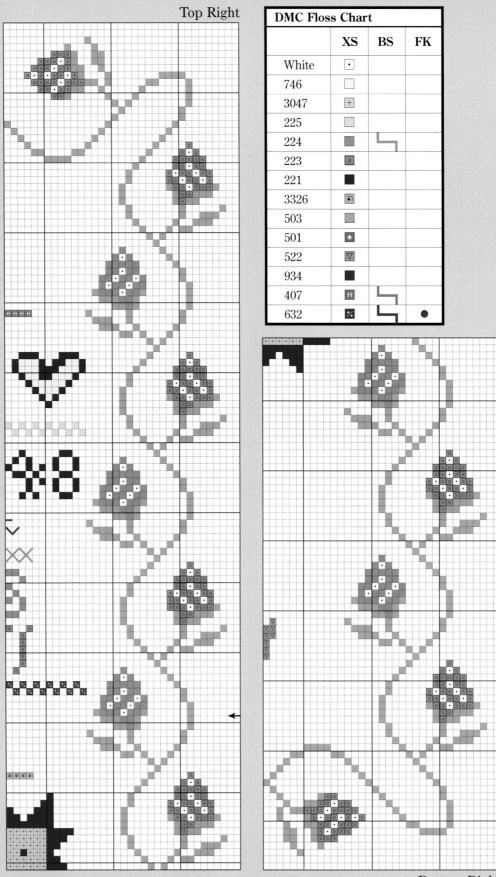

DMC Floss Chart

	XS	BS	FK
White	·		
746			
3047	+		
225			
224			
223			
221			
3326	⊡		
503			
501	★		
522	▽		
934			
407	H		
632	▨		●

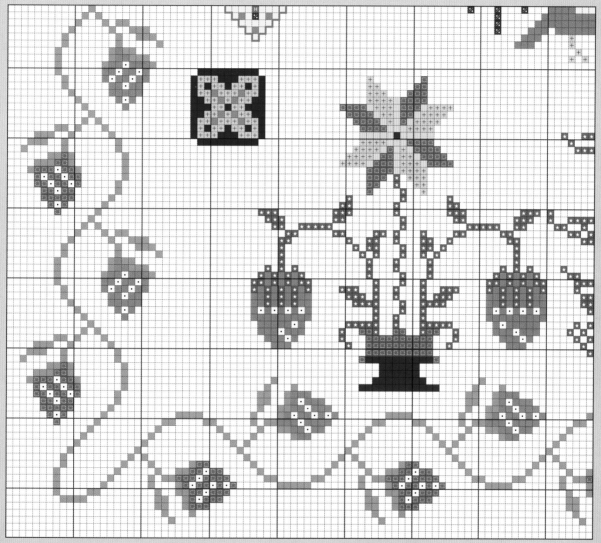

Bottom Left

Bottom Center

The sampler text reads:

this work in hand my friends may have
when i am dead and in my graw
and when the bell for me dose toul
sweet Jesus chris recive my soul
mary marsdens work ased 15 1803

This Sampler was made by
Mary Marsdene Pincock,
Mother of the late John Pincock, in the year
1803,—126 years ago, when she was only
15 years old.
Donated to Daughters of Pioneers by
the John Pincock Family February 22nd.
1929

VINTAGE CROSS-STITCH SAMPLER

STITCHES

he needlework stitches featured in the following pages have been used throughout the book in various projects—all of which you can replicate at home. Although machines have eased the burden on homemakers to supply by hand the needs for clothing and decorative items for the home, none of the charm of handwork need be sacrificed. Joys of needlework as a worthwhile pastime include the meditative as well as the practical.

BACKSTITCH

1. Insert needle up through fabric at A, using three strands of floss.

2. Go down at B, one stitch length to the right.

3. Come up at C, one stitch length to the left.

4. Go down at A.

BULLION LAZY DAISY STITCH

1. Insert needle up through fabric at A. Keep ribbon flat, untwisted, and full.

2. Go down at B.

3. Come up at C, but do not pull needle through.

4. Snugly wrap ribbon around needle tip one to three times. Holding finger over wrapped ribbon, pull needle through ribbon and down through fabric at D.

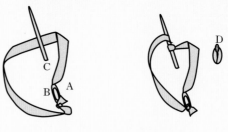

BUTTONHOLE STITCH

1. Insert needle up through fabric at A, using three strands of floss.

2. Go down at B.

3. Come up at C, keeping floss under needle.

4. Go down at D. Repeat.

CASCADE STITCH

1. Thread ribbon on needle. Allow ribbon to twist. Go down at A.

2. Come up at B and go down a C, making a small backstitch to hold cascade in place.

3. Come up at D. Repeat for deired length.

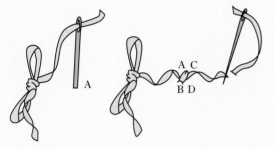

CONTINENTAL STITCH

1. Insert needle up through fabric at A.

2. Go down at B, the opening diagonally across from A.

3. Come up at C and down at D. Repeat.

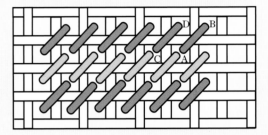

COLONIAL KNOT STITCH

1. Insert needle up through fabric at A. Drape ribbon in a backward "C." Place needle through "C."

2. Wrap ribbon over needle, then under tip of needle, forming a figure-8. Hold knot firmly on needle. Go down through fabric close to A. Hold ribbon securely until knot is formed on top of fabric.

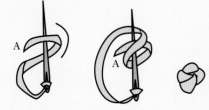

CORAL STITCH

1. Insert needle up through fabric at A.

2. Hold thread loosely on surface of fabric with opposite thumb.

3. Go over ribbon and down at B.

4. Come up at C and over ribbon again, forming a knot. Repeat.

Note: To alternate direction, change angles of B and C.

CRISSCROSS STITCH

1. Insert needle up through fabric at A at edge of fabric, but not through fabric.

2. Go down at B directly across fabric, dividing it in half.

3. Come up again at C, that will divide the fabric in half again, and go down at D directly across from second stitch. Continue to divide fabric two more times.

4. Come up in center of fabric and make two or three small stitches to hold down the intersecting stitches. Tie off ends at back.

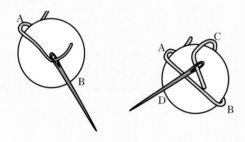

CROSSOVER LAZY DAISY STITCH

1. Insert needle up through fabric at A. Cross over to the right of ribbon.

2. Go down at B.

3. Come up at C and pull ribbon to desired shape.

4. Go down at D, making a small Straight Stitch to tack loop.

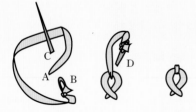

FEATHER STITCH

1. Insert needle up through fabric at A.

2. Go down at B.

3. Come up at C, keeping floss under needle to hold it in a "V" shape. Pull flat.

4. For second stitch, go down at D.

5. Come up at E.

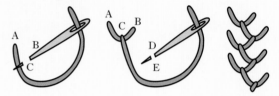

FRENCH KNOT STITCH

1. Insert needle up through fabric at A, using three strands of floss.

2. Loosely wrap floss once around needle.

3. Go down at B next to A. Pull floss taut as needle is pushed down through fabric.

4. Carry floss across back of work between knots.

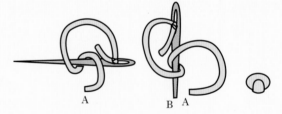

KNOTTED & LOOPED RIBBON STITCH

1. Insert needle up through fabric at A. Tie a knot in ribbon ¼" from entry point, or amount indicated in instructions.

2. Fold ribbon over on itself from knot. Stitch into ribbon and fabric directly next to entry point to complete stitch.

3. Allow entire knotted and looped ribbon to remain above surface.

Lazy Daisy Stitch

1. Insert needle up through fabric at A. Keep ribbon flat, untwisted, and full.

2. Go down at B.

3. Come up at C, keeping ribbon under needle to form loop.

4. Pull ribbon through, leaving loop loose and full. Go down on other side of ribbon near C, forming a Straight Stitch over loop.

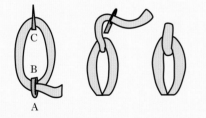

Loop Petal Stitch

1. Insert needle up through fabric at A. Form a loop in ribbon.

2. Go down at B, piercing ribbon.

Classic Hand-stitched Pillow

Loop Stitch

1. Insert needle up through fabric at A.

2. Go down at B close to A.

3. Pull ribbon part way through fabric. Insert a piece of drinking straw or pencil through loop. Pull ribbon snug to hold petal shape. Keep straw in place until the next petal is made in same manner, then remove pencil or straw. If desired, these petals can be tacked in place.

HEIRLOOM-STITCHED ALBUM

OUTLINE STITCH

1. Insert needle up through fabric at A. Keep floss to the right and above needle.

2. Go down at B.

3. Come up at C. Repeat.

POINTED PETAL STITCH

1. Insert needle up through fabric at A. Turn ribbon under at a 45° angle, then forward at a 45° angle to meet entry point.

2. Stitch needle into ribbon and fabric at B, next to entry point.

3. Tack or press ribbon point as desired.

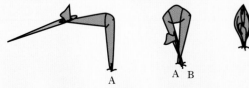

RIBBON STITCH

1. Insert needle up through fabric at A. Lay ribbon flat on fabric. Go down through ribbon at B. Slowly pull length of ribbon through fabric, allowing ends of ribbon to curl. If ribbon is pulled too tightly, the effect of the stitch can be lost.

2. Vary petals and leaves by adjusting length, tension of ribbon before piercing, and tension of ribbon being pulled down through itself.

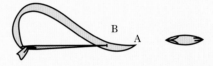

RUFFLED RIBBON STITCH

1. Insert needle up through fabric at A. Mark 2" from ribbon entry point.

2. Thread hand-sewing needle with matching doubled thread. Bring needle to surface at entry point. Gather-stitch along selvage edge of ribbon to the mark.

3. Pull gathers for desired stitch length. Insert hand-sewing needle back down through fabric, securing thread and gathers.

4. At end of stitching, pierce ribbon with needle at B.

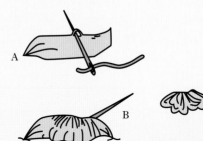

Antique Stitched Shelf Cover

Satin Stitch

1. Insert needle up through fabric at A.

2. Go down at B.

3. Come up at C, then go down at D, keeping stitches close together.

4. Repeat to fill design area.

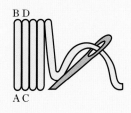

Slip Stitch

1. Work from right to left, holding folded fabric edge in left hand. Insert needle up through fold at A.

2. Go down at B directly opposite of A, catching one or two fabric threads.

3. Come up at C through fold ¼" from A along edge. Repeat.

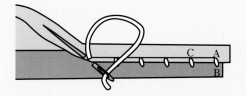

Stem Stitch

1. Insert needle up through fabric at A. Keep floss to the left and below needle.

2. Go down at B.

3. Come up at C.

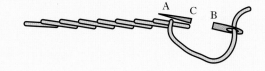

Straight Stitch

1. Insert needle up through fabric at A.

2. Go down at B.

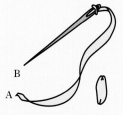

Twisted Ribbon Stitch

1. Insert needle up through fabric at A. Give ribbon a single twist to create a point.

2. Go down through ribbon at B.

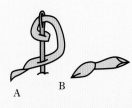

Vintage Ribbonwork Box

TRANSFERRING

Transferring and tracing of patterns and stitch guides is somewhat tedious and generally necessary. With today's technology available to needle artists in the forms of electronic copy machines with enlargement and reduction capabilities, electric light-boxes, computer scanners, and chemical transfer mediums for paper and fabric, securing designs where you want them—in their ideal sizes—before stitching is no longer a formidable task.

METHOD 1

1. If directions indicate to enlarge pattern, place pattern directly on copy machine. Enlarge pattern to required percentage and copy onto tracing paper.

2. Using craft scissors, cut patterns from tracing paper and place on fabric, cardboard, or poster board, following instructions such as: place on fold, cut 2, and so on. Using craft or fabric scissors, cut out pattern pieces.

METHOD 2

1. If directions indicate to enlarge pattern, place pattern directly on copy machine. Enlarge pattern to required percentage.

2. Tape photocopy onto window or light-box. Place fabric over photocopy and using fabric marker, trace around pattern. Transfer any markings onto fabric.

METHOD 3

1. If directions indicate to enlarge pattern, place pattern directly on copy machine. Enlarge pattern to required percentage and copy onto tracing paper.

2. Using craft scissors, cut patterns from tracing paper and place on cardboard, then secure on one edge with transparent tape.

3. Slip a piece of transfer paper, between cardboard and tracing paper. Trace over design, using an inkless ballpoint pen. Use a light touch, as pressing too hard can dent cardboard or make marks that are difficult to cover.

4. Lift off tracing paper and transfer paper.

ABOUT THE AUTHOR

*W*orking with vintage pieces of fabric, lace, and other representatives of fine needlework has long been one of Mary Jo Hiney's favorite mediums. Mary Jo took up needle and embroidery thread at the age of three, sitting next to her mom as she sewed. She began to work with vintage pieces when she first ventured out into the free-lance arena some 25 years ago and had the distinct pleasure of creating one-of-a-kind pieces of clothing for the tiny "Apple" boutique in Sherman Oaks, CA. But even before that, so many women shared with Mary Jo the treasure, history, and purpose of needlework through example.

Mary Jo Hiney continues to work as a free-lance author and designer in the fabric and craft industry, gladly sharing skill-filled secrets gathered over a lifetime of experience. She is an expert seamstress and credits her solid sewing foundation to her mom, who had learned to sew in junior high from a very strict teacher. Mary Jo's designs focus on gifts and decorative accessories, her one-of-a-kind pieces display beauty always enhanced with function.

DEDICATION:

For Auntie Carol: For teaching me the value of good manners and the joy in loveliness.

ACKNOWLEDGMENTS

We would like to offer our sincere appreciation for the valuable support given in this ever-changing industry of new ideas, concepts, designs, and products. Several items shown in this publication were created with outstanding and innovative products developed by Lina G's at 468 Morro Bay Blvd., Morro Bay, CA 93442 (805) 772-7759 www.linagtrimsandribbons.homestead.com

A special thank you to Ned and Margaret Favero and Phyllis Roger who graciously allowed us to photograph parts of this book in their homes. We would also like to thank the Weber County Daughters of Utah Pioneers Museum for allowing us to photograph items in their museum. Their trust and cooperation with displays and collections of memorabilia from the time of the earliest settlers of the area in 1848 are greatly appreciated.

Weber County Daughters of Utah Pioneers Museum is located in Ogden, Utah. The museum building has served the community continuously since 1902. Built by and for pioneer women using Sunday butter-and-egg money, gleaning the fields, each being assessed five cents, plus volunteering labor it still took twenty-five years to complete. Dedicated in 1902, the building served as the social center of Weber County. In 1926 it became a museum dedicated to pioneers. In 1942 it became a day-care center for women who went to work for the war effort. Then in 1945, it again became a museum.

METRIC CONVERSION CHARTS

mm-millimetres   cm-centimetres
inches to millimetres and centimetres

inches	mm	cm	inches	cm	inches	cm
⅛	3	0.3	9	22.9	30	76.2
¼	6	0.6	10	25.4	31	78.7
⅜	10	1.0	11	27.9	32	81.3
½	13	1.3	12	30.5	33	83.8
⅝	16	1.6	13	33.0	34	86.4
¾	19	1.9	14	35.6	35	88.9
⅞	22	2.2	15	38.1	36	91.4
1	25	2.5	16	40.6	37	94.0
1¼	32	3.2	17	43.2	38	96.5
1½	38	3.8	18	45.7	39	99.1
1¾	44	4.4	19	48.3	40	101.6
2	51	5.1	20	50.8	41	104.1
2½	64	6.4	21	53.3	42	106.7
3	76	7.6	22	55.9	43	109.2
3½	89	8.9	23	58.4	44	111.8
4	102	10.2	24	61.0	45	114.3
4½	114	11.4	25	63.5	46	116.8
5	127	12.7	26	66.0	47	119.4
6	152	15.2	27	68.6	48	121.9
7	178	17.8	28	71.1	49	124.5
8	203	20.3	29	73.7	50	127.0

yards to metres

yards	metres	yards	metres	yards	metres	yards	metres	yards	metres
⅛	0.11	2⅛	1.94	4⅛	3.77	6⅛	5.60	8⅛	7.43
¼	0.23	2¼	2.06	4¼	3.89	6¼	5.72	8¼	7.54
⅜	0.34	2⅜	2.17	4⅜	4.00	6⅜	5.83	8⅜	7.66
½	0.46	2½	2.29	4½	4.11	6½	5.94	8½	7.77
⅝	0.57	2⅝	2.40	4⅝	4.23	6⅝	6.06	8⅝	7.89
¾	0.69	2¾	2.51	4¾	4.34	6¾	6.17	8¾	8.00
⅞	0.80	2⅞	2.63	4⅞	4.46	6⅞	6.29	8⅞	8.12
1	0.91	3	2.74	5	4.57	7	6.40	9	8.23
1⅛	1.03	3⅛	2.86	5⅛	4.69	7⅛	6.52	9⅛	8.34
1¼	1.14	3¼	2.97	5¼	4.80	7¼	6.63	9¼	8.46
1⅜	1.26	3⅜	3.09	5⅜	4.91	7⅜	6.74	9⅜	8.57
1½	1.37	3½	3.20	5½	5.03	7½	6.86	9½	8.69
1⅝	1.49	3⅝	3.31	5⅝	5.14	7⅝	6.97	9⅝	8.80
1¾	1.60	3¾	3.43	5¾	5.26	7¾	7.09	9¾	8.92
1⅞	1.71	3⅞	3.54	5⅞	5.37	7⅞	7.20	9⅞	9.03

INDEX

Acknowledgments 126
Antique Pintucked Dress . . . 25
Antique Stitched Shelf Cover
. . . . 123
Baby Shoe Pincushion . . . 13–14
Backstitch 118
Beaded Keepsake Holder
. . . . 107–109
Bullion Lazy Daisy Stitch . .118
Buttonhole Stitch 118
Cascade Stitch 119
Child's Napkin Apron . . . 34–35
Classic Hand-stitched Pillow
. 121
Colonial Knot Stitch 119
Continental Stitch 119
Coral Stitch 119
Crazy-quilt Sewing Case
. . . . 46–49
Crisscross Stitch 120
Crocheted Edgings 106
Crossover Lazy Daisy Stitch 120
Cross-stitch Remembrance
. . . . 110–116
Dutch Laundry Sack 26–30
Elegant Cutwork Cloth
. 80–83
Elegantly Beaded Purse
. . . . 50–51
Embroidered Sundress
. . . . 31–33
Fancy Felt Pincushions . . 38–43

Feather Stitch 120
Floral Accent Box 96–103
Floral Embellished Pillow
. . . . 84–89
Fluting 100
French Knot Stitch 120
French Seam 20
Heart & Tulip Bag 60–67
Heirloom-slip Pillow 18
Heirloom-stitched Album
. . . . 122
Introduction 5
Knitting-needle Keeper
. . . . 56–59
Knotted & Looped Ribbon Stitch
. . . . 120–121
Laminate 101
Lazy Daisy Stitch 121
Loop Petal Stitch 121
Loop Stitch 21
Lovely Lace Towels . . . 104–106
Metric Conversion Charts
. . . . 127
Monogram Embroidery 74
Monogrammed Memory Album
. . . . 73–77
Narrow Hem 23
Organza Pintucked Pillow
. . . . 19–25
Outline Stitch 122
Picture-perfect Redwork
. . . . 70–72

Pointed Petal Stitch 122
Ribbon Stitch 122
Ribbonwork Bouquet . . . 90–95
Ruffled Ribbon Stitch 122
Satin Stitch 123
Sewing Tool Keeper 10–12
Slip Stitch 123
Stem Stitch 123
Stitches 118–123
Straight Stitch 123
Timeless Mantel Cloth . . 78–80
Toddler's Smock 36–37
Transferring 124
Trapunto Boudoir Envelope
. . . . 52–55
Twisted Ribbon Stitch 123
Vintage Crazy-quilted Footstool
. . . . 49
Vintage Cross-stitch Sampler
. . . . 117
Vintage Cutwork Tablecloth
. . . . 82
Vintage Needlework . . . 68–117
Vintage Pincushion 14
Vintage Pincushions 15
Vintage Quilt Kitchen Items
. . . . 55
Vintage Quilting 44–67
Vintage Ribbonwork Box . . 123
Vintage Sewing 8–43
Vintage Sewing Hutch 12
Vintage Tuffets 16–18